BECOMING EGOLESS

A MARTIAN'S PERSPECTIVE ON LIFE

ARE YOU WORTH THE EFFORT?

BY marc (the Martian)

DEDICATION

This book is dedicated to Alvan, who introduced me to the world of educational/self-help and inspirational reading and to Carol, who provided a convenient test case to study and apply some of these ideas and who helped with the nuts and bolts of creating the finished product.

I would also like to thank all the actual creators/producers of such informative materials. Once we have decided that we are worth the effort, the process of self-improvement and ego awareness is quite logical and simple.

TABLE OF CONTENTS

INTRODUCTION   i

CHAPTER 1: SELF-HELP READING   1

CHAPTER 2: THE ELUSIVE AND POWERFUL 1%   14

CHAPTER 3: TIME, HEALTH AND MONEY   25

CHAPTER 4: BALANCE OR MODERATION IN ALL THINGS   59

CHAPTER 5: THE ELUSIVE AND POWERFUL EGO   72

CHAPTER 6: SLOW DOWN AND THINK MORE   86

CHAPTER 7: MAKE HAPPINESS AND FUN A DAILY PRIORITY   93

SUMMARY   105

INTRODUCTION

After more than two decades of study, introspection, and lots of quiet thinking, I've come to feel just like a Martian wandering among very busy earthlings. I didn't start out this way. It all happened through observation/awareness and asking a lot of questions and trying to understand the motivation behind the actions of my fellow earthlings. Why do they do what they do? What drives them? Why do so many people seem unhappy and unmotivated? Why are we so distant to each other? What happened to common respect for each other? Who says we have to work the best 40 years of our lives under someone else's control at a job that may be soul destroying and unfulfilling? What happens in the "Golden Years", when your physical body starts paying the price for all those "working years"?

I had hundreds of questions as a young man but few answers or even a plan to get the answers. Today, I have fewer questions and perhaps a few answers which I hope to pass on to help other people on their life journey. I am as special as you are and have no super learning powers other than my own amazing, creative, problem solving mind/brain. However, I have created a lot of free time in my life, thru acquired knowledge, to quietly reflect/ponder the mysteries and often insanity in our human world. I started out near the bottom and with the help of my creative computer mind/brain, began the process of reading, learning, and incorporating new skills and knowledge into my life. I was just one of the "insignificant 99%" with no special skills or talents when my own life's study began. I have had a lot of time to think and reflect and analyze our world because of my acquired knowledge of money and health at an early point in my life. I have studied and analyzed my own life path more than most to discover the likely root of that learning curve.

I have created a simple, uncluttered life with lots of free time to think and reflect and improve daily. As a result, the odds are now in my favor for ongoing improvement into the future. Very few things in this life are guaranteed with the exception of death and taxes. But you can still tilt the odds in your favor by doing some fairly simple actions on a daily and ongoing basis. You can make the same changes to your life. You have the same equipment or better already. There is nothing to buy, no get rich quick schemes, no special courses to take, no one else to rely on, no time constraints, etc. etc. There is some effort involved however, some work, some study and certainly some changes in your life as needed.

Are you worth the effort? Are you worth it? You already have the equipment needed and so all that is left to do is to get going at this new task. You just have to start right now. Just make the decision to try something new in your life. How have you been doing in life so far? How are things REALLY going for you? Perhaps you just need fine-tuning or a complete over-haul. You are in control of your thoughts and actions. The knowledge/personal power is there for the taking and is usually low cost or free. You already have the computer needed to use the acquired information effectively. Make the choice today to start getting some of that precious free knowledge to rebuild your life and increase your personal power.

What goes through your mind 1st thing in the morning after waking up? Are you going to do some exercises right in the bed before you get up? Are you going to get dressed for an early morning jog or brisk walk? Have you planned out your day to include some self-help reading, some exercise, some social or family time, and some relaxation and fun? The 1st decision for most of my Martian days is: am I worth the small effort to do these basic daily maintenance chores? That question will probably haunt you now that you have finally been asked. If you genuinely feel that you are worth the small effort involved, then you are probably already doing them. Or you could start doing these exercises tomorrow morning and take them off your to do list. No doubt, there will be many other daily decisions coming at you as the day progresses.

Trying to come up with a title to this book was a long and evolving process. As I gained new insight into the inner workings of what we call human life, my perspective kept enlarging and changing. The picture got bigger and bigger as my view of life encompassed more and more of daily activities, and then the cycles of life, etc. You start concentrating on your own little world and then the camera lens zooms out to view your local community, your town or city, your state or province, your country, your continent, your planet, solar system and so on. Each time your perspective changes, you see things more clearly.

As you grow in knowledge and increase your view of life, the interrelationships and interactions between the different levels become clearer. Everything is connected it seems! We are all connected in some mysterious way. As you learn more, your perspective rises higher and higher. It is like climbing a large tree when you are lost to get your bearings and see the way to go. When people say to look at the big picture when making important decisions, this is probably what they mean. You try to see the entire forest through the individual trees. Online maps sometimes have a zoom in or out function that shows this process beautifully.

My own childhood was similar to most and not noteworthy one way or another. It was neither up lifting or degrading but more like a kind of neutral, apathetic existence. My self-esteem and confidence were poorly developed. I heard the word "NO" a lot and generally received less than adequate interest or attention from my caregivers and other adult family members. I believe this basic scenario is typical of most childhoods in the developed world as opposed to the undeveloped. So far, I have little experience with the undeveloped countries of our planet. Some children have had it much worse and a lucky few had it better.

I am quite sure that most of these children did not feel truly valued, respected or honored as the magnificent beings that they really are. Probably they were a novelty at first and then less so as the years went by. If there were siblings to compete with, then their share of attention/value was probably reduced even further. The parents, when asked, usually state that they did the best they could at the time. I'm not sure what that answer actually means but you do hear it a lot. Parents are too busy, time is too short, life is too complicated etc. etc. Unfortunately, what is… is!

Reality is just the way things currently are. Reality is neutral and has no axe to grind as they say. If your current reality is bad, then you have the power and tools needed to change your life situation. The entire process of changing for the better starts with the simple decision to take some new actions starting today. We cannot go back in time to alter past events. We must play the cards we are dealt as best we can. Becoming aware of this early situation is a great 1st step in your future growth. If you just assume that you were somehow screwed up in your childhood; you are probably correct.

I certainly did not stand out in my formative first to fifth years. I also was not fortunate enough to have an interested mentor/life coach to help guide me as I grew older. This scenario is quite common nowadays, in my Martian opinion.

The formative years (1-5) become less than ideal to create a self-confident, mentally powerful and productive adult. We start to cover up our inherent magnificence with layers of life detritus and limitations. We forget what we started with. We forget what we are at our core. We are definitely NOT GARBAGE!! We are, in fact, quite magnificent and that includes all peoples of all races and colors throughout the planet. If you have a body and a brain, then you are already magnificent.

My own process of awakening began when I started reading about history and war in my early twenties. World history seems to encompass a series of endless wars, then reparations and some peace and then more destructive conflicts. This process is then repeated over, and over, and over again to the present day. I couldn't understand the purpose of these endless conflicts in the history of the planet. What drives us as humans to engage in such predictable and repetitive bad behavior? I was beginning to appreciate the creative, problem solving power of my own brain/mind. Asking questions and seeking answers wherever they may be is a process to be developed. Where do things like the Manifest Destiny Doctrine come from? How do we defend our actions against those indigenous people around the world and throughout the ages? We certainly destroyed a lot of property and killed or injured many people but what was accomplished? What changed in the short run? What changed in the long run? I had many questions, few answers, and much confusion.

In many ways, this book is about common sense. It also becomes a book about hope for our future. Is there a solution for most if not all of our major problems on this planet? Of course, there is. We all have impressive equipment to work with. Our equipment including body and brain are quite incredible if you don't know already. Many knowledgeable people believe that most of us humans are only using a small fraction of our potential power and skill. I certainly agree, based on what is happening around us on this planet. Lots and lots of insane actions and ignorance all over the globe are the current reality. When something beautiful or loving does occur on this planet, when we can come together without our egos getting in the way, you can get a glimpse of what is potentially possible. You must know or at least suspect what our potential is and that we humans as a species can do so much better.

Can we change? Can you change? Do you know of anybody who has actually changed? Yes, Yes, and I do know somebody who has changed and for the better at that. We actually have to change in this world of ours just to get by day after day. One of the few absolute facts of our existence is constant change and you are already doing it. We all live and function in an ever changing environment. We humans have no choice in the matter. Do you have the same job, same car, same house, same life partner, same neighborhood, same friends, etc. etc. as you did five years ago? How about ten years ago? I think you get the idea. We can change and we are doing it all the time.

Are you worth the effort? Are you worth the time to learn new approaches to life? Are you worth the time to study your ego and learn to take back control of this elusive and powerful force? These questions are tough to answer and of major importance. If knowledge is power and we would all like more power or control over our lives, then we should get some of that knowledge. If knowledge is power and access to knowledge nowadays is abundant and easy to get, then getting personal power should be easy. It is of course! Become a regular patron at your local library and start gathering some of that knowledge/personal power. The cost is minimal or even free. You can bring in books, CD's, or DVD's from many other library locations, if desired.

If you can read, the books are there to borrow. If you can't read, there are probably free classes at the library or they can steer you in the right direction to find the resources that are needed. All it takes is YOUR decision to make the effort. Are you worth this effort? You can even access the internet for free or low cost and open up a world of information on almost any topic that can be imagined. Health and money matters are covered in exhausting detail online. There are mountains of information to be read, studied, and eventually applied if you will just put in the effort required and pick the right topics to become an expert in. Those topics should include time, health, and money. You may start to see a pattern with many of my solutions or suggestions. They are of low cost or free.

As a Martian, I have found that most of the best things in our world are low cost or free. I hope to convince my fellow earthlings that this is the current reality.

Gaining knowledge is like a sponge soaking up information. Sometimes, it's a visual, auditory, or feeling process, but most of the time, it requires work. There is lots of reading and studying, rereading and highlighting, discussion, and finally implementation into your own life. It has been suggested that because we have two ears and just one mouth, we should spend at least double our time listening and not talking/lecturing. Try talking less and listening more to your fellow human beings. You will probably learn more and will show some respect to the speaker. You may also begin to notice how our elusive/powerful egos can create a hindrance/roadblock to our knowledge gathering activities. Our egos can become a powerful force preventing us from positive, creative change.

There are not many people who would argue that each of us is endowed with some really magnificent equipment to do this work. We each own outright a magical body and problem-solving mind/brain. Both of these items are uniquely constructed and already paid for. There is nothing to buy in this program, there are no expensive courses or qualifications required to get started. Your magnificent equipment is ready to be used and at your disposal as a healthy human being.

In our early childhood, we tended to give our newly developing bodies the respect and reverence they deserve. As a young baby, much of your new knowledge came from a naturally exploratory, instinctual nature. The baby has an unbridled curiosity and just plain joy in discovering her new environment. There were fewer limitations on where you could explore or when. There were fewer self- imposed restrictions on the process. You just crawled along and saw, touched, smelled, and even tasted whatever was in your field of view. This is a normal, innate, and healthy stage in the child's early development. You were that child once upon a time. As we got a little older, we may have started to appreciate the creative and problem –solving capabilities of our mind/ brains. When you look at a newborn baby, you cannot help but notice the perfection of form and the exquisite design within. How is it made? How was it designed? Who or what starts this mysterious and complicated process?

I will make a number of assumptions throughout this book including the following:

There is no black and white in human affairs because of our incredible complexity. We are all slightly different and unique with our own emotional baggage and life story. Everything involving humans is therefore a shade of grey. Many of us hope for a black or white answer to life's complicated questions but they rarely exist. There are no guarantees when it comes to human nature. Rather you simply put the odds in your favor by following some of these ideas. Why not stack the deck of life in your favor?

Much of life appears to involve simply good luck or bad luck but it is still nice to be able to influence the areas of your life that you can and improve your odds of a better future. I am amazed at how often a lucky break can determine a person's entire career. I am also shocked at how one piece or instance of bad luck can also destroy a life of work and effort. These unknown forces are out there and, as a result, should be influenced in our favor if possible. If you are prepared both mentally and physically when the good luck occurs, then the odds will be in your favor for a successful outcome. On the other hand, if you experience some unusual bad luck in your life, then your newly acquired expertise will still put the odds in your favor of a positive outcome. You will more likely survive this temporary setback, recover quickly, and get back in the game of life.

Some people argue that smoking is not harmful because their grandfather smoked for over 50 years and still lived into his 90's. Other people argue that their grandmother never did any aerobics in her life and she still lived into her 90's as well. There are no guarantees with us but you can certainly improve your chances with these simple concepts. Maybe you have a special smoking gene or exercise advantage but who really knows and why take the unnecessary risk? In some ways, things are very simple in theory. But, in practice, and particularly with human relations, things can get very messy.

Each one of us is a unique chemical factory with incredibly complicated interactions within. As a result, some of these ideas will work differently for each of us. You would like to become an EXPERT on you particularly in the area of health and well- being. The work and effort involved is an investment in you and that is very good. Prospective parents are not issued child raising manuals to assist them in such a huge responsibility of training fellow human beings. Creating self-sufficient, independent adults from children is a daunting task and a huge responsibility for prospective parents. We need to give such choices a lot more consideration, thought, and time to help insure a better outcome.

Our individual EGOS are stealthy, elusive and incredibly powerful influences on our everyday choices. Much of our behavior and suffering is related to our EGOS. In my Martian opinion, basically all of our suffering is due to our egos. Just the simple AWARENESS of the powerful influence of your EGO on most of your day to day decisions is a great first step. Our egos can be that powerful and that destructive. Your perspective of life widens as your knowledge base increases and you create a scaffold of sorts to build up a world view. Your viewing screen enlarges from your own life to family life, to neighborhood, to town or city, to state, to country, to entire planet etc.

As human beings, we each have an incredible, self-healing body and creative problem –solving mind/brain. These two facts alone make each of us magnificent! Is there any doubt concerning these two facts?

Fact #1:   You have an incredible, priceless, self- repairing body which is able to do physical work.

Fact #2:   You have an incredible mind/brain with unlimited creative potential and problem-solving abilities for the mental work.

We have these things at our disposal but few of us know it or remember it. Our upbringings, schooling, society, and the status quo certainly don't help matters any. Many people feel that it is normal for us to suffer as we go through life. The suffering we go through in this earthly life is preparing us for something greater in the future or so it goes. To many people, our life is like a training ground or stage to prepare us for a better, brighter future. So why use these tools at our disposal if we are expected to suffer and plod through our days on this planet while waiting patiently for the bright new mysterious next stage? Some of us are waiting patiently for this new and improved future. I am not. I disagree strongly with that idea.

If we have already been given these powerful tools, than why not utilize them to their upmost in this life as opposed to some future date and alternative life? What is the sense of having these powerful tools at our disposal if they are not going to be used? Why are we given this incredible equipment in the first place? As human beings, we have to REDISCOVER our inherent magnificence and take back control over these precious assets once again. When we start using our bodies and brains more efficiently again, it seems very likely (to my Martian way of thinking at least) that a lot of the insanity in the world today will diminish/disappear.

If we can become more aware of our ego's influence on our day to day decisions, then I feel quite positive about our future. Remember that there are no guarantees when humans are involved. If we as humans can evolve to a reduced or egoless state, then we will certainly reduce our suffering on this planet. This work is doable and is not some pie in the sky, Pollyanna, feel-good dream of a crazy optimist. When we finally make the decision and do the work, the results will follow. At least, we can put the odds in our favor for a better outcome in the future. We can certainly do much better with our health, finances, and time on this planet than we are currently doing.

The BIG Question is: Are we worth the effort collectively? Are you worth the effort individually? I hope the answer is a resounding YES!

CHAPTER 1: SELF-HELP READING

I got introduced to my first self-help literature in my late twenties. It was probably "Think and Grow Rich" by Napoleon Hill and the "launch sequence" of my life education was suddenly initiated. If you will just read, study, and apply such books in your life, how can you not improve your life situation, live more effectively and efficiently? There is no downside as far as I'm concerned (except possibly boredom??) but unlimited upside potential to reading and studying self-help books.

Remember:

Fact #1: You have an incredible, priceless, self- repairing body which is able to do physical work.

Fact #2: You have an incredible mind/brain with unlimited creative potential and problem-solving abilities for the mental work.

Think about the super computer Watson on the game show Jeopardy! IBM worked long and hard and spent a lot of money trying to duplicate the capabilities of our own human computers. The human brain has amazed doctors, surgeons and many other research professionals for as long as it has been studied. In some cases, scientists and medical professionals have devoted their entire working careers trying to figure out the mysterious workings of this small organ (2 or 3 lbs on average).

This 2.5 lb jelly mass that consists mostly of fat is made up of smaller components called neurons. These neurons seem to gather, organize, and transmit electrical pulses or signals to other parts of the structure. There are many BILLIONS of these neurons in each of our brains and yet most of the brain is plain old water. The average brain can be made up of over 100 billion of these units. That number is a one followed by a lot of zeroes. The number of possible connections between these neurons grows exponentially as you add more neurons to the mix. Two neurons gives two possible connections, four neurons gives 64 possible connections, six neurons gives over 32,000 possibilities. I'm sure you can see the incredible numbers involved here. The total number of possible connections between the neurons in your own brain has been estimated to be greater than all the known particles in the entire known universe. That number is beyond belief and yet we all have this incredibly complex tool at our disposal right now. Are you intrigued yet concerning your own brain?

The neurons continue to grow and organize themselves throughout our lives. Initially, it was thought that brain and neuron tissues could not grow and duplicate themselves but this has been proven false as we learn more about this magical organ of ours. The process of neuroplasticity suggests that this incredibly complex organ can reorganize itself as needed. In the developing baby or fetus, these neurons are being created at a rate of hundreds of thousands per minute. Ten minutes of time = over a MILLION new neurons created! The neurons communicate or talk to each other through something called synapses and each neuron can have thousands of these connections as well. These interconnections allow for unlimited variation and possibility of brain function among us humans. This helps explain the complexity when trying to predict human behaviour/ possible outcomes. The numbers involved in any discussion of the brain are enormous and we each have one of these organs already at our disposal and ready to be used.

The brain is supplied with hundreds of thousands of MILES of blood vessels to nourish and support its important role in our lives. As we progress through life, it was thought that the brain stops growing around age 18 to 25 but newer research has shown that sections of this amazing organ continue to grow and change with use.

The Cerebral Cortex is such an area that grows thicker and more complex as we use it. When you learn a new language, play music or memorize a map, new growth and complexity in the appropriate sections of the brain can be actually seen. Mental activity and thinking on a problem or situation will cause new neurons to be created. This process of continual neuronal growth takes place throughout our lives in response to mental activity. It seems that the brain does not stop changing or improving because of a specific age reached in your life. Do you feel more magnificent now?

When does a person learn about these brain characteristics and learning potentials? Did you know about them before now? Does it happen in their formative years (1-5) through the caregivers and adults in their life? This period of time would seem to be the most ideal for such knowledge. These early or formative years are a very important time in our brain development. As mentioned earlier, new neurons within the brain itself are being formed at a fantastic rate every minute even during early pregnancy. This is the reason for having excellent nutrition during this time in a woman's life. It is speculated that the newborn baby's brain will increase in size by a factor of 2 or 3 in the first year of life. It has been hypothesized that a stimulating environment provided for the child in these early years can result in a very significant improvement in their ability to learn for the rest of their life. Reading aloud and talking on a regular basis with your young child will encourage brain development. In fact, the basis for such emotions as joy, happiness, fear and shyness are already developed at birth and the particular style of nurturing that the child receives at this crucial time will influence how these emotions are modified further.

On the other hand, an environment with little mental stimulation during these early formative years can cause a major decrease in the ability to learn for the rest of that child's life. Studies have shown that child abuse at this time can actually retard further development of the brain and can permanently affect future brain growth and complexity. These comments stress the importance of using this early time to give the child the best odds of a fully functional brain.

How do you talk or interact with your children? Are your conversations uplifting and positive? Are your interactions with your children meaningful and do they make them think about and question things/status quo? The main purpose of parents, in my Martian opinion, is to produce happy, productive, and independent members of society. Are your conversations and actions with your children helping to create happy, productive, and independent adults? If you do not provide this valuable input, at this early stage in their lives, who will teach them?

If the early years have been sub-optimal for this brain development and learning, then is it likely to occur during public and high school education? What happens to us as we enter institutionalized school learning? What happens to the magic that we all knew before? What happens to that incredible body and mind/brain as we progress through our formal schooling period?

Are we likely to get it during college or university days? I certainly didn't get it and I think that most students do not. Gradually and methodically we forget about our incredible bodies and brains. We stop respecting them. It is almost like putting our body/brain into standby mode and never really turning them on again. We stop respecting our miraculous machines by not exercising properly and eating for nutrition. Do you really have to argue and analyze and intellectualize the bodies need for regular strenuous exercise and adequate, varied nutritional foods? Do you remember when extended bed rest was a viable and common procedure for sick people with broken bodies? How did that idea work out long term? I like the phrase: "use it or lose it" when it applies to our own bodies and minds. It all seems so sensible to my Martian way of thinking. This idea of using it or losing it should be common sense to us humans, but something usually happens as we progress through life to prevent it.

So where does that leave the young human in their interaction with life after the formal period of specified schooling? Life is a continually evolving and dynamic game. Constant change and mountains of new information are coming at you whether you are ready or not. I couldn't believe how impractical and of little use so much of my high school and later conventional education was. I knew virtually nothing about health, money, saving, investing, budgets, cash flow, buying a house, starting a business etc. etc. Common sense, instinctual knowing is slowly and steadily destroyed in us. We are slowly and steadily conditioned, on a daily basis, to become apathetic. We are bombarded daily by media experts to fulfill their agendas. Many of us are molded into robot-like zombies whose sole purpose on this planet is to consume, consume and consume some more!

We tend to seek constant and ever more complicated entertainment almost as a distraction or opiate to forget our magical gifts. We seek out drugs and alcohol to numb our uneasy feelings regarding our potentials. We are mostly sad and living desperate, quiet lives. Most people tend not to complain because who wants to bring others down and add to their misery. How many people understand the importance of time in our lives? We don't even know how much time each of us has in this life. And yet, how many people waste so much of this precious time complicating their lives with unimportant activities.

Most humans in the developed world are working hard to buy more things that they can't afford to impress others that they don't even like or care about. Many are over-working because of a lack of understanding regarding money, savings and investments, budgets etc. The concept of work flexibility and free time and even work choices is foreign to most. The idea of working part-time or choosing not to be paid to work at all, such as volunteering, would be a real stretch of their comfort zones. WE CAN DO SO MUCH BETTER! We can turn on our incredible bodies and minds again to reclaim our inherent magnificence and personal power. YOU ARE MAGNIFICENT. You just haven't been told that in a long while and you have probably forgotten.

This book is mostly about my own journey of rediscovery of my body and mind. If you will just RECLAIM your childlike-exploratory nature once again, then the marvellous can happen. If you start effectively using and fine-tuning your incredible creative, problem solving brain then you can't help but improve your overall life condition. This is a simple elegant solution to many of our current woes. It is low cost or no cost (respect money) and it can be implemented immediately (respect time)

Currently, I assume you already have problems, so just pick one problem and write it precisely down on paper. Then start reading and researching, studying, and thinking about this one written down challenge. Use the creative powers of your human computer to find a potential solution. Then apply the potential solution and see what happens. Take some notes, make mistakes, and make changes in your world and then REPEAT PROCESS over and over again until your problems are reduced in number and more manageable. Our long- forgotten common sense would tell us to identify the problem, study and research the problem, try a potential solution to the problem, make mistakes or find a solution to the problem, and then pick a new problem to work on. You will get better at solving problems with practise and, as a result, the number of problems in your life will decrease.

Start respecting your magical self-healing body again so it will be available to do the physical work needed. Fix a problem, pick another and fine-tune your approach if necessary. Restart your own process of self-improvement and self-discovery. You will be creating a self –improving spiral that is always going up and getting better and better. Each time you use your body and brain to solve problems and create a better life, you will get stronger physically and mentally.

Now contrast that self– improving, self-guiding process with what happens to the majority of us as we plod through life in a self–inflicted daze. Without self-help literature or a good mentor, most young people stumble along without direction or even a financial goal to pursue. Mistakes will be made and unfortunately many years can be lost before progress is ever made. You never get back those lost years so it's a tough error to make. All this discussion is leading to a major question. The million dollar question if you will.

Question: Why don't most people read, study and apply self-help literature?

Possible answers:
   a) They already know the material and their lives are running well (doubtful, I certainly don't see that out there in reality).
   b) They don't care to know because they just plain don't care about their lives or others. They are apathetic about their existence and they almost feel they deserve to suffer. They do not feel worth the effort to do the work. (This answer is more likely and fits better with observed results in society)
   c) People don't know that the material is out there to read and study.
   d) People think that they are above or superior to the ideas that are presented in the self-help literature (strong EGO influence).

Apparently when we were very young and not yet conditioned by society, we had a natural exploratory manner and an uninhibited sense of discovery. It has been observed and studied that the first sense to develop while a baby is growing in the womb is TOUCH. The lips and cheeks of the fetus can experience touch around 8 weeks and the rest of their body sometime around 12 weeks. Touching everything and exploring uninhibited was the norm. We are curious by nature and seek out the answers normally without fear or limitations. It's amazing to watch a young child interact with their environment without fear, totally focused on the moment and usually having a fun time of it.

Most of us lose these precious innate qualities as we age and move through life. I didn't feel very special after the 1st five years of life. Our parents and/or caregivers or other adult role models normally all try their best. But where did they learn these important skills from themselves? Did they learn from their parents or grandparents? As youngsters, we watch, listen, and many times pick up bad habits or life choices from those adults around us. We get older and continue watching, listening, and modelling the people around us. In a few lucky instances, young people will remember and retain their inherent magnificence but most do not. Most of us at this stage in life will start to feel insignificant and less special every day. We will start making life choices that give our personal power and control away to others. These other interests can include other people, corporations, political parties, religious groups etc. etc. who will be glad to take over your life and show you what to do.

We are told what age to start working and what age to stop, what kind of work to do and what schedules are involved. Suddenly you are working at a 9 to 5 job with weekends off and two weeks paid vacation per year for maybe 40 or more years. What happened to that delightful exploratory nature and learning process of your early years? You know the one that I am referring to: try something new, make mistakes, make changes and improvements and repeat process over and over again.

I understand that this simple process of learning is termed the scientific method and consists of asking questions and seeking answers wherever they may lead. If it doesn't work, then try something else. If it does work, then study the process and repeat it and refine it. Always you are improving in a series of mistakes, improvements, mistakes etc. I like the analogy of a self-guided missile that zigzags back and forth always correcting until it reaches its target. Apparently, modern jet airliners navigate much the same way through a constant series of course corrections until their final and precise destinations are reached. The jets are off course something like 90% of the time while they are flying but it is not a big problem because of the constant course corrections.

As humans, we also zigzag through our mistakes. Why do we even call them mistakes? We have just found an alternative way that did not produce the results we were looking for! Unfortunately, without self-help literature or mentors, we don't usually reach our end target which should be a healthy and happy life.

If the answer to the self-help question from above is "B" as I suspect, then why don't people care to learn such material. Why would someone not want to improve their playing of the game of life? One of the earliest self-help books for many of us is the bible. Even the bible talks about the Lord helps those who help themselves. One of the best ideas contained in many religious teachings is to "Know thy self". Take the time needed to get to know your-self better. Start creating some space in your daily schedule to learn about you. What makes you tick? What motivates you? What are your CURRENT strengths and weaknesses?

Part of knowing yourself would include studying and applying self-help concepts I hope. So you may start to see why I felt and still feel like a Martian. I was studying all these self-help materials and learning important concepts while only a few others seemed to be doing the same. I was making changes and making lots of mistakes in my own life. In my early learning years, I assumed other people were doing the same thing. It just seemed so natural to do and made common sense. I wondered then and still wonder today, what percentage of people actually read self-help/inspirational materials on a regular basis? The answer according to some experts is around 10% of the reading public. Most people (90%) do not read self-help materials on a regular basis. This statement would coincide with the current reality as I see it. If you choose to not read these materials, then how do you eventually get the knowledge/personal power and life control that is contained within? If most of us don't want to hear the advice from other humans due to our ego's influence and most of us don't read about it on a regular basis, then how do you finally get the information? I think you can start to see the problem we have in the developed world.

A lot of the humans that I interact with feel as though their education was completed after high school or college. There was just no need to continue learning new material so why even bother? Some of the best books that I have acquired on self-help were purchased for less than a dollar. That fact alone can show you how much the books are valued by our current society. It is through such reading that I have learned about money, health, ego, balance, simplifying life, setting priorities and living a more serene, uncomplicated, happy life.

I will share some of this material with you in the following chapters. It is hoped that this exercise will stimulate your own search for knowledge to improve your own life situation. After all, you have the same incredible creative problem-solving computer as I do. So let's get to it! We have identified a problem and now we will apply a potential low-cost solution.

The amount of self-help material available today is staggering in quantity and mostly of low cost or free to the user. This is a great reason to join your local library. So, once again, why do most humans not read and study and apply these materials as is evident in our modern world? We are so much greater than simple consumers who zoom around like robots getting stuff and working hard to make our lives miserable. In many cases, we actually work hard to make our lives miserable. We are so much greater than busy bodies accumulating money at all costs to buy things to impress people we don't even care about. We are so much greater than simple zombies stumbling through life always consuming and seeking expensive entertainment to distract ourselves from our current reality.

Why not try and change our current reality instead? Why do we make ourselves so busy with little time left to reflect on what's really important in our own lives? Why do we try to do so much in any given day? Many of us are frantically running all over the place and looking very busy but really accomplishing little. Multitasking does not work for the vast majority of us humans. In fact, all of the tasks attempted, will probably suffer in quality. We need to consciously create free space or buffers in our lives and use these created spaces to slow down, DE-stress, focus, and think more. Sometimes, just slowing down to think and reflect and start prioritizing your world will start this natural innate process of exploration once again. We all did it as young humans in the past. Make the mistakes, study those mistakes and make improvements. Apply these concepts and always refine and adjust the new information to fit into your daily routine. You will always be moving forward, and upward. You will become self-correcting until you reach your ultimate destination of awareness, serenity, happiness and freedom. You are just like that jet airliner we talked about earlier that was off course 90% of the time and yet still arrives at its final destination mostly on schedule and without mishap.

I have found that a DAILY routine that includes an hour or so of inspirational/self-help learning is very effective to reboot our mental systems. You can vary your DAILY routine with books on tape, books downloaded from the internet, or good old fashioned paper books. The key is to read DAILY and study and finally apply the concepts into your own life. Little daily baby steps will help build a better life for yourself and eventually for your family and others if you choose. I have met people who say they READ self-help and they certainly have an impressive library of such books to showcase. However, their knowledge is only superficial and they certainly are not applying the concepts described in their books. There is not much point in scanning or perusing such books without studying the material sufficiently to see its application in your own life and then ACTUALLY applying it.

If your typical day includes many hours of watching television, then find something interesting or inspirational to watch daily. I have always been a fan of PBS or public television. There is always something to learn on this channel whether it be cooking, crafting, documentaries, or world history. Another bonus of PBS is limited commercials mostly at the start of programs and usually no commercials once the program begins. Take one hour of your daily TV watching and simply change the channel to find your local PBS station. Start watching at least one hour of PBS daily and you will become familiar with their broadcast schedule including Nova, Front Line, Nature, POV, Masterpiece Theatre, and various children's programs, etc. etc. This television station of learning and entertainment will also give you an opportunity to donate monies to them and help assure the continued existence of such an important vehicle for acquiring new information and skills. You could then become a member of your local PBS and start putting your money/power into something you and your family find worthwhile. Television can actually become a powerful influence on your daily program of self - improvement. If you are already watching TV on a daily basis, you would simply change the channel and watch one hour or more of educational programming via PBS or something similar.

Reading self-help is different than reading a novel for entertainment purposes. Therefore, READ, STUDY, REREAD AND STUDY and finally apply something NEW in your life and watch what happens. Afterwards, MAKE CORRECTIONS and refinements and repeat process! You will always be moving upwards, always getting better day by day. Each one of us is truly magnificent. We should never forget that. It is a basic fact of our very existence!

If you would like to share some of your favorite self-help books or materials, please e-mail me at martianmarc@gmail.com. If you would like to know what my top five self-help books are currently, please e-mail me at martianmarc@gmail.com.

TO SUM UP:

In my Martian world or way of thinking, you would:

Read daily one half hour or more of inspiration and/or self-help books. Become a regular patron of your local library to access free materials and/or the internet.

Watch one hour or more of PBS to break up your daily TV entertainment and learn something new.

Start thinking about   TIME<HEALTH<MONEY   and the proper order for these three major concepts.

Study the material, test yourself or have someone test you.

Try teaching the material to someone else to see how well you actually know it.

Finally, apply and start using some new ideas in your life. See what happens and make adjustments to fine tune your new habit.

Do something different NOW!

REMEMBER YOU ARE WORTH IT AND YOU ARE WELL EQUIPPED TO DO IT.

Fact #1:   You have an incredible, priceless, self- repairing body which is able to do physical work.

Fact #2:   You have an incredible mind/brain with unlimited creative potential and problem-solving abilities for the mental work.

CHAPTER 2: THE ELUSIVE AND POWERFUL 1%

We hear so much lately about the 99% of our society. We don't hear as much about the other 1% however. The "insignificant 99%" obviously includes most of us and has been studied and talked about widely especially since the 2008 recession/correction. We are born into this world and typically have weak formative (1-5) years which lead to weak later years and decreased creativity, exploratory natures and the asking of questions and seeking of answers. We are beaten down by life and slowly lose our natural enthusiasm, curiosity and innocence. We become fearful and limited and closed minded. We are ruled by outdated opinions, outdated religious views, outdated societal roles.

The 99% start making bad choices such as:

- Overspending on traditional education, buying a home with a large mortgage, buying a car with a large loan, buying anything with a loan or credit cards.
- Spending money that we don't have and therefore can't afford to waste, starting a family early before some financial stability and maturity is in place, working a job that is deadening to our souls and our inherent magnificence.
- Consuming too much, too fast, and slowly destroying the planet and its other inhabitants.
- Working for 40 or more years to pay for all those things that we couldn't afford to impress people who really couldn't care less about us.
- And then finally reaching the "Golden years" of retirement when many of us rely on outside financial assistance such as company pensions and government to help us eke out an existence until death mercifully stops the game.

From my own Martian perspective, I find this process depressing, pathetic and insane and yet I keep seeing it happen daily. Is there any wonder why I feel like a Martian wandering among very busy fellow earthlings? We are magnificent beings with incredible brains/minds and amazing self-healing working bodies. That elusive 1% has the same equipment as us (assuming they are still human of course). Do they have different or modified mind/brains from us? Are their human computers superior to our 99% models?

Just what is the difference between the 1% and the other 99% of us?

Modern science and technology can't duplicate the brains function or the body's incredible operating systems and each one of us already owns the equipment free and clear and ready to work. It has been estimated that the human brain can hold over five times as much information as the entire Encyclopedia Britannica. The storage capacity of the human brain in electronic terms is thought to approach 1,000 terabytes of information. To put this figure into some perspective, the National Archives of Britain which contains over 900 years of history only takes up to 70 terabytes of electronic space. This would hardly put a dent in your own brain storage capacity. And yet, this incredible organ seems to operate on the same energy as a simple 10 watt light bulb. Even when we are sleeping, our brains are generating enough energy/watts to power a small light bulb. How is this possible? Are you impressed yet?

Some of the nerve impulses that communicate within the brain can travel in excess of 170 miles per hour. This fact would help explain your quick reaction to a stubbed toe or pinched finger. The high impulse transmission speed within the brain helps to explain this reaction time. And even though the brain typically makes up around just 2% of our body weight, it uses more oxygen than any other organ in the body. It has been estimated to use approximately 20% of the oxygen that enters your bloodstream.

Finally, just when you thought you knew it all, your brain is much more active AT NIGHT than during the day. When you go to sleep, your brain wakes up and turns on. Brain Researchers still do not know why this is but you can now appreciate the importance of a good night's sleep. So if we have the same incredible brain equipment as the elusive 1%, then what is the difference in actions between the 1% and the rest of us?

As a Martian, I suspect that one answer to this important question is a healthy respect for money and what money can do for you. The 1% knows that money makes this world go round and that money is alive. The 1% has a deep respect for the power and potential influence of their money. It is almost always about the money. Money is not as important as health or time, but it still fills the 3rd spot in an impressive group of concepts. Follow the money trail when you are trying to understand some world process or unusual trend. Maybe we have found the reason for wars throughout the earth's history.

I was always fascinated by world wars and smaller distant conflicts like Korea, Vietnam, Kuwait, Iraq and Afghanistan. Who benefits, who loses? What is ultimately accomplished? In my Martian opinion, very little is ultimately accomplished and much returns to normal or even worse after some time has passed. Yet, our history is filled with a series of wars and conquests and more wars etc. Some of these conflicts have been going on for generations and still show no sign of letting up. It is pretty obvious who loses in these conflicts. Young men and women in their prime of life, children, and young families as collateral damage, entire cities are extinguished and disappear all as a result of war.

So now on to the tough question, who benefits from war? Is there really some group of individuals who actually gain from these wars? As I have said earlier: follow the money when you are stuck trying to understand a complicated process in your backyard or around the world in some distant country. Who accumulates money during these repetitive conflicts? Some of the obvious and not so obvious beneficiaries are defence contractors, weapons and ammunition makers, all types of suppliers and manufacturers for the soldiers and their gear. Which group of people owns or controls these entities? Is it the 1% or the 99%?

In past years, the country's dictator or ruling family or select group of generals etc. could benefit directly from war. Some family dynasties apparently got their start by lending money to the warring nations. The elite or 1% can be very creative when it comes to making money in any world situation. Why can't we, the other 99%, do it? The point is there are benefactors to these seemingly insane and costly events. Follow the money and you may start to understand what is behind the event. Follow the money and you can start to understand the motivation for such colossal energy expenditures and waste.

In general, the 1% can benefit and the other 99% can pay the ultimate price in terms of life. Knowledge is power because you start to understand what is driving the process. I am going to guess, that because the elusive 1% benefits from these conflicts in some way, that is why they continue with some regularity throughout the planet's history. Now what do you do with this potential answer? Study it and think on it and think some more and look for the common thread joining all these world events.

Think about the flow of money from one country to another or from one government to another etc. Money makes the world go around. The 1% knows this, benefits from it and continues to amass more and more money and more control and power as a result. The 99% doesn't generally know this and continues to suffer the consequences of this ignorance. Less and less money and reduced control and power are the inevitable result for the 99%. What is…is!!

What can we do about this? What can we change in our own little lives and family to reverse the process and stop the growing gap between the Haves and the Have nots? My Martian answer is to start developing a deep RESPECT for money and what it can accomplish. Become an expert on money. Become an expert with your money. Learn all there is to know about money, savings, interest, dividends, capital gains, cash-flow, mortgages, budgets, etc. Start to create some free space in your day by establishing a money cushion or buffer. Are you worth the effort?

I bet the 1% has already done this financial study. Start reading and studying about money, budgets, net worth, good debt and bad debt, investing etc. etc. If you work to earn money, then what do you do with that precious money you just worked so hard for? Do you put some savings from each paycheck in your local bank or investment account? Most people do not even do this. Do you deposit 5% or 10% of your earnings or more? Just what is the purpose of work? EXACTLY why do we work?

Are you working just for fun or to meet new people? Maybe after you have accumulated a sizable portfolio with a nice monthly cash flow, then you could choose to work for fun or to meet people or just to get out of the house. INITIALLY, you should work to build up your cash or liquid assets. In my Martian world, you INITIALLY work to earn and save money! You initially work to earn, save and invest money. In LATER years, it is hoped that you can work for other reasons then just accumulating money but, at first, it is all about the accumulation of money. Show me the money at first and I will show you some options later on.

At that future point in time, you will take a chunk of that earned money and INVEST it for yourself. How much will you invest? The answer is: how fast do you want out of this work cycle/slave wage period of your life? As a Martian, I like to invest 15% to 25% or more of my earnings because I know the importance of this invested money. If I earn $100.00, then I would invest at least $20.00 for myself. I would put the minimum needed in my bank/checking account for practical every day bills, etc. and then INVEST the rest for myself and family.

Why do I emphasize INVESTING your earnings as opposed to saving? Saving typically generates interest income which currently is at very low historical rates. A depositor at a bank will earn virtually zero on your savings at the present time. A skilled investor can earn 5 to 10 to 25% or more annually depending on your developed skill set at managing your portfolio. You can read about and study such savvy investors once you start your own financial research.

That collection of investments that you have created and carefully managed will then start doing some MAGIC just for you. More on this later! Your bank currently pays you little or nothing on your savings or checking accounts. Now what do you suppose the banks do with your deposited money? The banks are experts on money. The banks know intimately the time value of your money. This is what the banks do for a living. The banks will gladly take your money/savings and they will INVEST them as best as they can. They are very good at this investing most of the time and consequently the banks can and have become some of the richest, powerful and most influential corporate entities. Some of their top employees are probably members of the 1%.

Study these banks. Read a book or two on the banking systems and how their business is operated. Do you think that your deposited savings just sit there in your account doing nothing, earning nothing and not being reinvested in something else by the banks? THINK AGAIN! If you were an expert with money and people handed over their paychecks to you every week or couple of weeks, what would you do with this wind fall of free cash? You just might pay those depositors a little weenie bit for the use of their money and the rest would be smartly invested just for you. Start doing exactly what they do. They are EXPERTS at investing money. You can become an EXPERT at investing your own money!

Do some research on the banking system and their strong lobbying groups, political influence, and the financial power they have. Imagine a business where people bring you their money for free basically. You would gladly accept it and hopefully thank them. Then you use all of your expertise to invest this FREE money which was given to you. You would naturally earn a good return by INVESTING that money and not being too greedy so as to cause a recession/depression (2008-present day). You then pay the depositors very little for the use of THEIR money and pocket the difference.

I read somewhere that you can forget about robbing a bank to get money. It is much smarter and efficient to OWN a bank and get all that money and more legally. The banks provide a needed service for holding/protecting our bank accounts and allowing us to write checks for monthly bills, use debit cards, Visa/MasterCards etc. We need that service so just put the MINIMUM needed to run your monthly checking account and YOU invest the rest. You do the investing of your money for yourself and family. You become the money expert that most banks have already become.

Do some research on bank policies, bank fees, bank reserves, and the reserve multiplier and the information may startle you. It certainly startled me. We are playing a game that is rigged for the house to win. The house (banks) has the playing odds in their favor. Let us re-balance the game somewhat and become EXPERTS with our own money and investments. Study the rich, study the 1%, duplicate the good things they do and throw out the rest. Take the good qualities, refine them to yourself and make them your own. Learn from the actions of the 1% and meld the good qualities into your own life. You can custom create a new money savvy person because you are magnificent. Remember Facts 1 & 2!! The 1% knows that money is alive. The 1% knows that most debt is bad to your net-worth, that cash flow is KING, that compounding of interest is the 8th wonder of the world, and that every single monetary transaction must be given RESPECT.

Can you guess what kind of debt is good debt? Is there really a kind of debt that is actually good? Just keep reading. Make your money work for you for a change. Make every earned dollar productive and don't waste the power of these greenbacks. Properly invested money is alive in the sense that it will generate offspring in the form of dividends, capital gains, and interest. Once you have created a nest egg of investments or portfolio, that portfolio can start to magically produce free monthly cash flow for you and your family to use. As long as you don't kill the golden goose (your nest egg or portfolio), you will continue to receive regular golden eggs (monthly cash payments). I hope you won't use this knowledge to create or influence another war but by understanding a reason for war maybe we can reduce the occurrence of these wars in the future.

If money is the reason behind these world events, then study money and become an expert with your own finances. If you do not take control of your own money, then others will gladly fill in the void to your detriment. Take the good (respect of money and its ability to create and control) and leave the rest behind (world wars and regional conflicts). Emulate the good of the elusive 1% and discard the bad. I look at the 1% as worthy of study and emulation. The 1% of our society is not the enemy and, in fact, they can serve as role models for the rest of us. They are surely impressive with their earnings. They create and control world events, they have power and influence and yes they have money. Let's learn from them and use their knowledge of money in a new way; a more balanced and non-destructive way, a building up as opposed to a tearing down.

We can create a new and healthy respect for our money! Money is ultimately power, freedom, choices and control etc. We must learn to respect our money better. We must learn to make each of our earned dollars work for us instead of always working for someone else. If the 1% of our society (including banks) is already experts with money, then we must learn to become experts with our own money. Are you worth the effort? After all, it is YOUR money we are talking about!

My Martian way of thinking differs from the status quo when it comes to just how much money you need to be happy. How much do you need to have some flexibility and choices in life and to enjoy the good things? How much is enough? I bet the amount is much less then you think. There are already many books and studies out there on this very topic. Start reading and learning and do something different with this new knowledge. If you will develop a deep respect for your money, if you analyze each financial transaction as being important to your health and happiness, you will find that less is more. There will be less complications, less time wasters, less busy, less buying and consuming, less eating out and instead more quality time, more enjoyment with people, more respect for people, more conscious consuming and purchasing, more meals at home with family and friends etc. etc..

We seem to be on a paradigm of more is better where there is never enough. How much is enough? Is having more always better? We keep amassing more and more things which require more and more of your precious limited time on this planet. If you ate out at your favorite restaurant every day instead of every month or special occasion, what happens to this experience? What happens to most things when they are enjoyed too much? Usually, the experience can become routine, boring, and not so special any more. We should practice moderation/balance in all areas of our lives. We may actually have to limit ourselves so as not to destroy the magic of those events. Don't we have to limit the frequency of eating at our favourite restaurant to maintain its special status? We have to consciously limit these special events to keep them special.

It is like the law of supply and demand where too much supply of an item naturally reduces the demand for the item concerned. Doesn't a monthly or quarterly or special occasion in your life to enjoy a meal out make more sense? Do we actually have to pace ourselves and limit our expensive entertainment? What do you think? What happens to many of our wealthy movie stars, sports idols, or music artists who have it all?

Too much of anything tends to reduce its being special. If there is too much supply of something, then the price of it normally goes down. Too much food tends to make us overweight. Too much water even leads to sickness. Too much alcohol could lead to alcoholism. Too much leisure points the way to poor physical health. Too much buying causes reduced savings. Too much productive time, wouldn't that be a nice problem to have! Not likely at this point in your journey but I think that you get the idea.

Moderation in all things is a nice easy rule to live by and it certainly makes common sense. If there is a limited supply of something, then the price or value of it normally goes up. As consumers, we can consciously limit our spending in certain areas to maintain the value and its being special. We should strive for a balance or moderation in the primary areas of our lives including physical, mental, social, nutritional, financial and spiritual.

Do something physical each day. Read something inspirational/self-help each day. Try to engage and respect other people each day. Reflect and think about each day as it comes to an end. What worked well today? What didn't work as well? What improvements could be made tomorrow? What couple of things would you like to accomplish tomorrow and what changes would you like to initiate? Start using your incredible mind/brain and body to create the life that you want. Remember you are magnificent! You have the same equipment as the 1% but we seem to have forgotten how to use it. Change up your routine and try something new and exciting using that incredible problem-solving computer between your shoulders. Start to do the work today, do it NOW!

TO SUM UP:

In my MARTIAN way of thinking, you would:

Study, think about, and mirror the good qualities of the elusive and powerful 1% on this planet.

Emulate their good qualities such as a deep respect for money and its power to create and influence world events and global trends.

Read and study and read some more to understand the game of accumulating money quickly, then to magically investing that pot of cash to create your own monthly cash flow and individual pension plan. There is a massive amount of free information out there on this topic.

Join your local library and read the books for free and use their considerable resources to acquire knowledge.

Keep thinking about   TIME>HEALTH>MONEY   and the proper order of these concepts.

Research and read about banks and how they operate with your deposits to become powerful and influential corporate entities.

Finally, your money will start to work for you via dividends and capital gains instead of you always working for your money. What a concept to imagine! Every month or quarter, your investments (accumulated money) magically create free cash for your use and you do nothing except continue to stay alive in order to accept and use the free cash flow generated. The staying alive part of the equation is our next topic of discussion. You want to stay healthy and long-living to enjoy that wondrous personal pension that will be created. And that's where the second life priority kicks in, namely your health.

CHAPTER 3: TIME, HEALTH AND MONEY

What is the most important and precious thing in your life?

Have you ever asked and reflected on this question before? What is the #1 priority in our lives?

Where should you devote a majority of your thinking, study and creating? What is your best guess? The title to this chapter should give up the answer.

TIME

With my Martian way of thinking, the answer is clearly TIME! We do not know how long we will be on this planet. We do not know when our "game of life" is over. Except in suicide, we do not control the end point which could happen today, this week, this month, this year or whenever. Accidents, disease or global events could end your time/existence at any moment. What a tough concept to accept but absolutely true. Live each day as if it could be your last on earth.

How many people do you personally know or have heard of who suddenly change their lives for the better when faced with a life-ending diagnosis such as cancer? How many people suddenly get serious about time management once they finally realize that there may be a specific end date according to their doctor or care giver. In many cases, they will suddenly change some of their previous bad habits. They may stop wasting precious time on superfluous complications and trivial accumulations of more stuff.

How many times have you heard a long-time smoker or drinker suddenly get the will power/confidence to quit only after their doctor has told them that they must? Why does it take the doctor's warning to finally cause the person to change? How come the two-pack a day smoker for 30 years couldn't figure that out sooner? How many cigarettes did he or she have to smoke before this information suddenly popped into their consciousness? We are talking about thousands and thousands of individual cigarettes being lit, slowly smoked and then extinguished over all those decades while being apparently unaware of the damage or risk to their precious time on this planet.

Would you say that this person is knowingly committing slow suicide? Were these people dreaming or unconscious all that time? Some experts say YES they were and, in fact, they have a lot of other humans for company. Misery loves company. Some authors claim that around 99% of all people in the developed world are in fact unconscious as they plod through the motions of their daily lives. We seem to be conditioned on a daily basis to give up personal power/control over our futures. We are becoming apathetic and uncaring about most things in our lives and on this precious planet.

The first time that I had read that, I was shocked. I put the book down and started thinking, analyzing, and wondering about such a possibility. Could the vast majority of fellow humans be operating in a zombie-like unconscious manner? Why would they do this and why would they continue doing it until death ended the process? These are intelligent people with that incredible body and mind/brain thing I keep mentioning and yet they are seemingly plodding along in an unconscious dream. What is the reason? What is the answer to this million-dollar question?

From my Martian perspective, they HAVE SIMPLY FORGOTTEN about:

Fact #1:   You have an incredible self-healing body able to do physical work.

Fact #2:   You have an incredible and creative, problem-solving mind/brain for all the mental work.

They have stopped respecting themselves and have stopped caring at all. Could this explain our current weight and nutrition problem in society? How many diet books do you have to read to get the general idea of adequate, nutrient – dense foods and exercise to control weight? Could this explain our many world problems? They have forgotten the inherent magnificence that they were born with. They have forgotten about their own incredible, paid for computer-like problem-solving and creative mind/brain. It is still there and always has been.

The mind/brain is waiting to be used again. It just needs your awareness of it and commands and instructions to start up again. Turn it on again! Fire it up from its long dormant state. Dust it off and get ready to put it back to work. It's really just this AWARENESS of Facts #1 and #2 that starts the ball rolling and makes you fully conscious in your life again. With that new awakened perspective, you will develop a heightened awareness of your life. That newly found awareness could then lead you to the ultimate truth about Time.

Time is the #1 priority in all of our lives. Time is not controllable. Time can't be stopped or slowed down. Time is non-negotiable. No matter how much money that you accumulate you still can't directly buy or influence Time. Think about it for a long while and then start respecting your own time from this present moment onward. Always keep in mind the three life priorities. TIME, HEALTH AND MONEY and periodically check yourself on how you are currently respecting these items in your own life. Are you wasting precious time doing less important things? Are you looking after your health on a daily basis? Are you getting some physical exercise daily? Are you getting some strenuous exercise once in a while? Are you feeding your body good nutrition and a suitable number of calories to match your current activity level? What is your weight like? Are you happy with your weight? Do your favorite clothes fit nicely or are they getting a little tight to wear? Before you go out to buy bigger sized clothing, stop and think what is happening to your body. Do you matter enough to make a change? Are you worth the effort? If YOU don't care about yourself, then who is going to care for you? Are you worth it?

A daily assessment of your life priorities (time, health and money) will keep you on track and always trending towards ongoing improvement. If you need help in one area, ask someone knowledgeable (a mentor?) or start reading and educating yourself. Knowledge is power so start getting some of that power and control in your life. Read and study and apply something new to your life. Try it out and make changes if necessary.

Become an expert on time and your health and well-being. Become a money expert, an astute investor and start building your net worth year after year. Emulate the good qualities of the 1% and watch and learn from them. Money makes this world go around so naturally become an expert on money. Start respecting your money and your financial decisions more. You have worked long and hard to earn this money, so don't waste it on endless expensive entertainment/distractions and the accumulations of more and more stuff. You can do this. You are magnificent. You have an incredible body and mind.

Think about it. Reflect on it. How does that fact alter your concept of money and the endless quest for more things? Accumulating piles of useless stuff complicates your life and can make you so busy that you can't even think about how to stop the madness. Most of us keep ourselves so busy doing nothing important, that there is little opportunity left in the day to reflect upon our limited time and our use of it. Time is precious. Time is limited. Time is uncontrollable.

At the end of the evening, as you are lying in your bed, you can replay the day's events in your mind. Watch the movie of your day and see what worked and what did not. What changes could you make tomorrow? What would you like to accomplish tomorrow? Pick a couple of the most important things you would like to have done. Maybe, you need to make a list. Concentrate your thoughts on those important items like a laser beam and use your creative problem-solving human computer to find simple and elegant solutions for tomorrow's challenges. If nothing else happens, you will probably fall asleep and then leave your unconscious to keep working on the problem. This scenario sounds like a win-win to my Martian way of thinking.

Start living your life as if this day could be your last day. It really could be. What's more important than the unknown amount of time each of us has in this existence? How do you want to spend it today? Do you want to waste a lot of your precious time running around trying to multi-task and yet not really accomplish anything significant? Always remember that you are truly amazing and powerful. With such magical equipment at our disposal, we can all do so much better. You already have a priceless self-repairing body that can do amazing feats. You already have a magical creative problem solving mind/brain. Are you worth the effort to start using your powerful tools once again? They are just waiting for your command.

HEALTH

Closely related to the importance of time is the knowledge of health and our incredible self-repairing bodies (fact#1). In order to build up my case for the human body, here are some tidbits of information. Every day of your adult life, your body produces hundreds of BILLIONS of new cells. That is a lot of cells! This production requires energy from food to constantly repair and create new cells to form the various organs and tissues in the body. This is one of the reasons for carefully choosing good quality food and good nutrition at all meals.

While all of this production is taking place, we also shed over 500,000 particles of skin every hour or so. Hundreds of MILLIONS of our cells will die in our bodies every MINUTE. Even though that sounds like a lot, it is still just a fraction of our total number of cells which have been estimated at 20-60 TRILLION. Are you getting impressed yet? Are you feeling a little more magnificent now?

Just like the brain, the numbers involved are staggering and yet they accurately reflect what we already have. Over 30 million bacteria cover each square inch of your skin but thankfully most of these are harmless and some of the bacteria actually help with maintenance tasks. You may have read or come across the idea that we remake and rebuild ourselves constantly cell by cell. Imagine a self-repairing self-duplicating machine that you own. We shed and regrow our entire outer skin layer almost monthly. Your skin protects the internal organs from the outside environment and subsequently it dries and flakes off on a regular basis.

I hope that it is becoming obvious that your health and caring for your body's needs is of critical importance. Always remember, that once you have created your investment portfolio and it is producing a regular monthly income, you want to be around for a long time to spend this monthly bonus. Imagine having the money and the good health to enjoy it for a change. You can't control freak accidents and global events such as world wars, but you can certainly influence your own personal health. Creating a healthy body and strong immune system will put the odds in your favor when exposed to a disease or surviving a freak accident. Your physical strength and cardio endurance can make the difference in surviving an accident for instance.

If a strong flu virus suddenly appears and is making many people around you sick, then your strong immune system will put the odds in your favor of not catching it. Everyday common colds can be reduced in frequency and in duration if you create a more powerful and responsive immune system. Because our bodies are so complex, it is always about the odds of getting sick. As I mentioned at the start of the book, when it comes to human beings and their individual chemical factories, there simply are no black and white answers. You read and research and put the odds of staying healthy and strong in your favor. There are no guarantees to be made and each of us is a totally different complicated organism. Each of us can react differently to a standard drug or vaccination. Control what you can control such as nutrition and exercise and take direct responsibility for your health.

Even genetics play a smaller role in our overall health then was originally thought. I have read that your genetics and family history may only make up to 15 to 25% of the total influence on your overall health. Personally, I am hoping that family genetics are a minor influence on my own health because they are not favorable on their own. What do you suppose makes up the rest? Would you believe LIFESTYLE CHOICES! What you chose to do to yourself on a daily basis has the greatest effect on your overall health and longevity.

We all know or have read about wealthy people who have lost their health and would pay anything to get healthy again. How about losing your health in the endless pursuit of money? The unbalanced pursuit of money can certainly cause mega stress, poor nutrition, and lack of needed exercise. It would be such a shame not being able to enjoy the money if and when it does come. It has been estimated by experts in the field that over 75% of diseases are caused by or are complicated by STRESS. Stress is like a silent killer that most of us give little thought to. Pursuing work and money in an unbalanced way could certainly elevate your stress levels into dangerous areas. These are some of the reasons that health is more important than money in the grand scheme of things.

If you pursue money at the expense of your health, then you could actually die early or suffer years of sickness even though you are rich in monetary terms. You certainly are not helping your own health outcome. You are not putting the odds in your favor so to speak. So what do you do? Is there a simple, elegant solution to this problem? Why not try to balance the pursuit of money (which is necessary) with a deep respect for the health costs involved in the pursuit? Learn to work smarter, not harder and always save some money from every endeavor or job that you have. You work and you save and invest money always! Why are you working otherwise?

You should become an expert on money and how to spend it efficiently. That way, you can reduce the amount of time required to create your own personal pension or cash-flow and consequently save your long-term health in the process.

You can free up more time or space in your daily life with the cash cushion or personal pension. Money would then become less distracting to you and your family. Then, you can focus more attention on your health and physical body.

Your body is an incredible self-healing, self-replicating machine and yet it needs very little to operate efficiently. In fact, you could remove a major part of your internal organs and still survive. I am going to guess or hope that this research was done during our many world wars and other human conflicts. Apparently, it is possible to survive with the removal of the stomach, the spleen, up to ¾ of the liver and intestines, one kidney, one lung, and almost all organs from the groin and pelvic area. In some ways, our bodies seem so delicate and sensitive and yet under different circumstances so robust. Do some movement or exercise daily with a variety of intensity levels. Balance your exercise with light and strenuous bouts or sets. Some experts call this style of training "BURST TRAINING" and apparently it is more efficient and certainly quicker than the more conventional 30 to 45 min routines.

I think we all need some strenuous workouts which are balanced with lighter activities like walking or you can walk faster or uphill to change up the effort and our resultant pulse rate. Mix it up always! If you do a strenuous activity one day then take the next day as a resting and self-healing break. Our bodies are designed to move and do work. If sweating or perspiring is an ideal way to release toxins from the body via our skin, then get out there and create some sweat! It seems, nowadays, that we will spend a lot of money to reduce our movement and our work as well as complicate our lives and reduce our net worth. We are often working hard to screw things up.

As an example, I'm thinking of all the riding lawn mowers that are being sold to reduce our workload and make our lives a little easier. However, with the shiny new time saver to do the hard work, we will miss out on the potential physical exercise that could be gained. We wastefully spend our money, complicate our lives and miss out on the good feeling of working physically to accomplish something.

How is our current system working with all these labor saving devices? Do you remember when the idea of extended bed rest was an accepted medical procedure or protocol? How did that work out? What kind of shape is the typical

American or Canadian or European in? Sometimes we really do work hard to screw things up! Sometimes we work hard to make our lives more difficult. Oftentimes doing nothing would be much better than complicating our lives further. Just imagine working hard at something and yet actually making things worse. You would be better off staying in bed and doing nothing!

Read, study and think about it. Why would you pay to exercise at a gym when you could get exercise pushing a mower up hills and around obstacles for free and maintain your lawn at the same time? You will also gain the pride and feeling of accomplishment and control of doing it yourself. We need to move and work our muscles and breathe hard and sweat to maintain and respect our physical bodies.

Our skin is the largest detoxing organ we have. The skin can release various environmental and food toxins through the pores via perspiration/sweating. As a result, sweating on a regular basis is a good thing and inactivity or sedentary activities are not. It's your body, incredible and paid for but like most things it requires respect and care and knowledge of its workings. The decision to buy a riding lawnmower, as an example, shows how we can unknowingly complicate and disrespect our time, our health, and our finances. If you actually do manage to save some time with your new riding lawnmower, then I hope that you use that precious saved time in a productive manner such as an extra physical workout and not more sedentary TV watching.

Instead of all this complicated stuff, why not try my Martian way of doing things? What about this scenario: you buy an inexpensive or second-hand regular gas push lawnmower from your local garage sale? This purchase can actually help out a neighbour and keep the money locally. The cost could be less than $50.00 used. You could also buy the cheapest new one from your favorite local store (cost = less than $125.00 new). You use the lawnmower yourself and get some needed exercise either light or strenuous depending on the speed of cutting and the terrain.

Look for creative ways to have a workout and get some of your home chores done at the same time. It's a win-win situation! If you want more of a workout, look to do your neighbor's lawn or someone you haven't met yet and make their day a little easier. You could pay it forward as they say. You just might meet someone interesting and at the same time you will be improving the social component of your life.

I think the key is always to use your creative abilities to figure out more and more win-win scenarios. Find the simplest, most elegant solutions by THINKING. Slow your life down and think! Your body wins and your chore list wins and your neighbors win etc. etc. In my Martian world, that solution is a win-win. Respect your physical body and its needs. Respect and develop your creative ability and mind. You are magnificent. You are one of a kind. These are facts! Read, study and think about it.

Your health is crucial to your quality of life. The range of activities available to you is reflected in your physical power, endurance, cardio output, flexibility etc. Your immune system is constantly under attack from germs, viruses, toxic chemicals, stress etc. You don't feel like doing anything when you are sick or run down and without energy. Who would want that? Who wouldn't want peak health, peak physical power and endurance and a peak operating immune system?

But, you ask how do you get these precious things? What are the costs involved? I've found these things available for FREE via libraries and internet and other information sources. You can read, study, and think about these precious qualities of YOUR life at any time. So who wouldn't want these priceless items? I assume most if not all people would desperately want good health, strong bodies and powerful immune systems. Yet few people seem to have these things particularly as we age into the forties and fifties and beyond.

In my experience, I see a lot of preventable sicknesses such as, colds, flu and general malaise. I don't see many people respecting their bodies and general health. What do you see out there in your world? If you were given, free and clear, a classic red Ferrari valued at $250,000, how would you treat it? Would you read the manual? Would you study its workings and needs? Would you keep it clean and maintained and operating at peak efficiency?

I assume and hope the answers to these latter questions are a resounding YES. Well, think about it, your body and its abilities are worth much more than that Ferrari. So why wouldn't you respect it like it deserves? Study health books and nutrition guides. Find out what foods are good to eat and which foods to avoid or at least reduce consuming. Learn about sugar and its many negative effects on the body and the mind. Read about the 7 main triggers of food allergies including milk or dairy, peanuts, soy, wheat, sugar, eggs, and corn. Learn about wheat and gluten and its myriad effects on digestion, joint pain, mental function and weight gain.

Study and read, and learn about the insulin response to all foods including the glycemic index and glycemic load of foods. Determine which foods to avoid and which to consume more of. The information is available free of charge in books, audio books, videos at libraries or maybe even your well-read and knowledgeable neighbor or friend or family member. Join your local library and start gathering some of that pile of free knowledge/personal power and control over your life. Ask and you shall receive! Is your health and general fitness worth it? Are you worth the effort?

The main point as always is to read and gather this information together so as to better operate your body and build up and maintain your peak health and strong immune system. If you don't do it for yourself, who will? And what kind of a job will they do compared to your potential expertise and obvious familiarity with the object in question (YOU). Respect your health. Respect your body. Do the necessary work and reap the fabulous rewards for yourself. You deserve it. You are magnificent and one of a kind.

It's amazing to me as a Martian, how few people understand their health and the daily requirements of their bodies. Such things as getting adequate rest or sleep, reduced or controlled stress, proper nutrition, proper eating habits, food combinations that work and foods to reduce or avoid completely. I'm sure you have heard the stories concerning wealthy people whose health begins to fail prematurely and how they will spend everything and anything to regain this second most precious of our needs. They may have all the money a person could want but not the priceless good health that can be achieved or, at least, influenced. Health is more important than money. Without good health, what can you do with all that money and how can you bring yourself happiness and joy?

Once again, the amount of information available to all of us concerning health and wellness is staggering. The information is also free if you use your creative faculties such as libraries and the internet. Health is an area that can be studied and learned about via countless articles, books, documentaries, videos etc.

It is a huge and quite complicated or cumbersome topic that must be mastered to ensure a long, productive and happy life. An educated and interested patient has got to be a huge benefit if and when you require a doctor's help. Part of your one hour or more daily self-help reading must include health information.

As our environment is being made more toxic daily via new and untested chemicals, we must study and learn the health implications of this new toxic world. How are these new chemicals affecting us? How are these new toxins affecting our many bodily systems such as production of hormones, heavy metal accumulations, and immune function? The overload of toxins will certainly increase the stress on our bodies and likely lead to more sickness and cancers.

As things get more complicated day by day, we have to continually update ourselves with the new developments in our foods such as newly created additives, sweeteners, preservatives etc. Basically, the people making these new foods are experts and therefore, we as consumers must also become experts in our food choices. You are dealing with food experts so you have to defend yourself and your family with your newly developed expertise. As long as there are experts out there trying to separate you from your hard earned money, you have little choice but to get more knowledgeable in the appropriate areas. Otherwise, they will do what they feel is necessary and you will suffer the consequences.

Surely you have heard of fellow humans who catch a disease or a cancer and then begin to study and read everything on the topic. Suddenly, they can become as knowledgeable as your local doctor or even become world experts. How did they do it? How do these normal ordinary humans suddenly become world authorities on any given topic? They are human, the doctors are human, and the world experts are human. What is the difference between all these humans and you? Is it simply motivation? Is it just doing the required work/research? They must have felt that the effort involved was worth it. Do you?

You may find that our modern, complicated and fast-paced world will force us to become experts in many different fields. For instance, how does your body react to artificial sweeteners and other unknown chemical combinations? How does your body react to environmental toxins from our air, water and soil? What are the short term effects that we may experience such as drowsiness and mood changes? What are the long term effects? Are these effects even known or studied? Are you willing to take the chance with your health, your precious and irreplaceable wellness, energy and immune function?

How many chemicals are out there already that have never been studied for human short or long term effects? The answer is thousands and perhaps, hundreds of thousands according to my Martian research. What about the large number of brand new man- made chemicals appearing in our world daily? You could start your research on this topic with a book like: Rachel Carson's "Silent Spring".

There is a lot to read and learn and study and apply but you are now learning on a daily basis how to make better food choices and how to improve your overall health. As far as I can tell and have read about, it seems that almost everything health wise goes back to nutrition or what you eat. You are what you eat. What you put in this incredible body will certainly affect what comes out. Your body is a mass of chemicals interacting with each other to create this incredible human machine. Whatever you ingest with your regular meals has a direct impact on this exquisite chemical balance. Isn't this just common sense?

If you put low quality fuel into a Ferrari race car, it is not going to operate very well and the vehicle will certainly be functioning below its potential performance. If you put in garbage or poor quality computer code, the computer will not function as expected. The same process is operating with your priceless machine which we call a body. Poor nutrition, excessive empty calories, lack of needed vitamins, amino acids, and minerals and your body will likely suffer as well. If you think that all is well at the moment, then just give it time for the damage to show up in your physical being. Most of us humans can do almost anything destructive to our bodies and brains in our 20's and 30's. However, after that age, the odds are going to be against you and your continued good health. Maybe you are blessed with good genetics, maybe not, but why take the chance with your priceless health? When the potential solution is easy and low cost, why not put the odds in your favor of having excellent health for as many years as possible?

Too much sugar consumed and there are chemical ramifications to your body. Too many carbs and your body will react in predetermined ways as well. Too much protein, too little good fat, too much bad fat, too many calories for the energy expended or even too much food or the wrong kinds of food and suddenly you notice your clothes are fitting a little tighter. You have to loosen your belt a notch or two. You have less energy left over to do other things. Your normal daily schedule starts to change as you basically eat, sleep, work and veg out in front of the TV or other passive and sedentary entertainment.

The trend continues, more weight gain, less energy, less drive, less interest but now more sickness, more complications and more suffering. How do you stop this destructive spiral? Why not start reading some free books on the subject from your local library? You can also start reading and researching specific web sites or online articles from experts in the field. Education and Knowledge is power when applied properly. Start gathering some of that free knowledge/power and incorporate it in your new life. Otherwise, the new information is just more facts and figures. Read, read, and read some more until you become fluent with nutrition and the needs of your body to operate most effectively. AND THEN APPLY THIS NEW INFORMATION! Make some mistakes and make some changes towards always improving your life situation and personal control/freedom.

Remember:

Fact #1:   You have an incredible priceless, self-healing body for physical work.

Fact #2:   You have a magnificent mind/brain with unlimited creative potential and problem-solving abilities for the mental work.

Your body is an individual and complicated chemical factory. Your body may not react the same way as your mother or fathers or siblings or spouses. Build a solid base of nutritional information and watch or become highly aware of how certain foods affect your mood, your energy or your sleep quality.

When I eat regular pasta using white or whole wheat flour or regular noodles, I tend to feel very lethargic and sleepy afterwards for many hours. I also get stuffed up or congested and have trouble breathing through my nose. I am aware that this effect is not normal for my body after a meal. My body with its complicated digestive machinery and regular pasta are a bad food combination. How does your body react to eating pasta? Why this effect occurs after I eat regular pasta can be studied and determined or I can just choose to reduce or eliminate regular pasta intake. If I cook rice pasta as opposed to regular or whole wheat pasta, I don't suffer the same after affects. I don't like to suffer needlessly, so I simply reduce or eliminate this particular food from my food choices.

Sometimes, as an interesting experiment, I will have a regular pasta meal just to see if the after effects on my body are the same or worse as before. It is also important to remember that your complicated body is continually changing so doing periodic self-checks is helpful. Unfortunately, as we age many of our bodily systems work less efficiently as before. You can't see as clearly as in your youth. You can't see up close or as far away as in your youth. Your hearing is not as acute and you may lose the ability to hear high pitched sounds for example. As well, your taste and digestion and elimination systems also typically degrade with advancing age. If you pay attention, if you remain aware, and if you operate primarily in the now moment, you will notice these changes in your body.

As I entered my fifties, I certainly noticed that I couldn't consume the same amount of food as in my youth. I also noticed bloating and gassiness and a general uncomfortable feeling after eating most meals. The change in MY body chemistry seemed to occur relatively fast (one year time frame or so) but it did occur and it wasn't going back to the way things were. I had to understand what was happening to my digestive system to deal most effectively with the changes. Naturally, I started to read on the subject of aging and digestive issues that we may experience as we grow older. This new knowledge led me to make changes in the quantity and types of foods being consumed, the time interval between meals, and the combination of certain foods to reduce the bloating and belching after eating. Certain supplements like probiotics and pepsin and HCL seemed to help as well.

The fact was that my complicated body chemistry had changed (in this case with my advancing age) and I was prompted to seek new knowledge (through reading) to deal most effectively with this inevitable aspect of life. Human life consists of constant and continuous change. Will your body change at the same time? Will your body chemistry changes be the same as mine? Of course not, we are all complicated individual chemical factories. Just like fingerprints and snowflakes, no two of us are exactly the same. No two of us will react chemically the same either. The key is having knowledge of your own body and your own nutritional needs. What makes you feel the best? What foods allow you to operate at high efficiency? What foods allow you to sleep soundly and wake up refreshed and ready to go?

It is all so individually tailored to your specific genetic and chemical makeup, your current age, your gender, your stress level etc. etc. As you read about nutrition and start to expand your knowledge base, you will likely read about various common triggers that may negatively affect your health. Some people are lactose intolerant and cannot digest milk and milk products very efficiently. Some people are deathly allergic to peanuts or soy products. Other common negative triggers to be aware of include peanuts, gluten, wheat, corn, sugar, eggs and milk. These items may cause havoc with your chemical factory and gum up the works so to speak. Sometimes it is the foods you most enjoy that are causing you distress and an avalanche of physical and mental problems.

Most of us take the easy way (we think) with our health. We are constantly looking for that magic pill or potion that will suddenly and easily repair all of our ills and pain. It has been suggested that we are just basically lazy as humans and are therefore always looking for the easy way out of things. We don't want to do the work, the studying, the learning and the applying of new knowledge directly related to our medical condition. Your doctor has done the required reading, studying and applying of new information. If she can do it, then why can't you? Are you worth the extra effort involved for your own health or the health of a family member or friend?

As an educated patient, you can work much more effectively with your doctor. You are respecting your doctor's time and talents by educating yourself in medical manners. You will speak more intelligently with your health care provider. You will work towards a quicker solution because that incredible mind/brain system of yours will be inputting data to the conversation as well.

I have read that up to 75% of doctors' visits are strictly related to non-medical manners. Sometimes the patients just want to talk, be reassured etc. There is little doubt that the loneliness of most people in the developed world is a contributing factor. Finding someone who is genuinely interested in your life story and your problems may be worth the trip to the doctor's but you will be taking time away from other truly medically sick patients. Just imagine what could happen to those long waiting room times if these same patients educated themselves more, took more charge of their health, and took more responsibility with their health. The patient certainly wins by respecting Facts 1& 2.

Ultimately the patient should be more knowledgeable of their specific ailment and the likely causes and effects. After all, it is their specific body that is being studied. They can now take a more direct role in the solution and recovery. The doctor meanwhile has more time to devote to critical medical problems with other patients, who have also armed themselves with medical knowledge, nutrition etc. Everything would start to work much more quickly and efficiently. If we reduced or eliminated the 75% of visits to a doctor that are for non-medical reasons, then just imagine what could happen to the health care challenges and long wait lines we are currently facing. We each have an incredible creative and problem solving mind/brain just waiting to be used again to make our lives more efficient, happier and longer.

Have you ever heard of medical cases where the new parents have a very sick child? The child has a rare disease or an unknown disease and medical solutions or information is very hard to come by. Typically, the parents try everything that the medical establishment has to offer. Many doctors are consulted, many procedures are tried, much money is spent and much time is lost. The child's condition does not improve and may actually deteriorate further. The medical establishment has offered its best currently available solutions to no avail. The parents have exhausted most of their options and sometimes most of their money. It is at this point in time, that a choice is sometimes made. The parents can give up and hope for the best or the parents can become their own doctors, they can become their own solution. The parents can choose to fully engage their creative problem-solving mind/brain and start doing their own research and testing. They can read and study everything available on the subject including alternative medical procedures. Sometimes nutrition is a huge contributor to their child's ailment and they can study and analyze all of that information as well.

Eventually you have one or two highly educated and motivated people working 24/7 for the child's recovery. Can you just imagine what is possible NOW? There are published cases where the parents become world experts on a particular disease that had affected their child. I watched an older movie recently called: "Lorenzo's Oil", which tells a true story about two such parents and their son. The spouses have learned important skill sets on their own using that same incredible problem solving brain that we all have.

What did it take to make this happen? The answer is motivation, determination and a no-fail attitude. The point that I'm making is that these ordinary parents did this. They transformed themselves into experts, sometimes world experts by using their incredible problem-solving and creative mind/brain. Because they couldn't find a solution at this time to their child's ailment, the parents simply created a new solution and developed skills and procedures that could now be passed on to other people who come across similar challenges. This happened to ordinary regular people just like us. If THEY can do it, then why can't WE? Why can't we develop ourselves and build skill sets to help us get through life more efficiently, more healthy and with more happiness?

The parents mentioned previously were highly motivated. They were dealing with a suffering child and potentially life or death implications. That fact pushed them, forced them into action. If they didn't provide a new solution, who would? When would the solution come about without their dedicated efforts to speed the process along? As a Martian, I read and watch these things occur and wonder why we can't all do the same in our own life situation. The fact is we can do it but we seem to be lacking the motivation or determination to improve ourselves. We have become apathetic, we feel helpless and unable to change the outcome of our day to day lives. But if just one person has improved and built themselves up into a world expert on a particular subject, then it must be possible for all of us. What is so different between the newly created expert and the rest of us?

They had and still have a mind/brain similar to ours. They had and still have an incredible self-repairing magnificent body similar to our own. We seem to lack the awareness of these two facts. We have forgotten what we were provided with as newborns. Most of us have lost the instinctive happy exploratory problem-solving mode of living that we were born with. Why did this happen? Why is it still happening? What is the hold up towards a more intelligent way to live? I hope to provide some insight into just those questions.

The parents who become world experts to save their child are a shining example of what is possible for all of us. The example also highlights the importance of our health in the grand scheme of things. Without our health, even our incredible mind/brain does not function at peak capacity. If you don't have your health, it is certainly more difficult to earn money and the money you do earn may then be needed for medical supplies or services. How many people would give all their money to get back their precious health? How many people would pay anything to live another week, month or year? Unfortunately, many of us take our health for granted and unless we get sick, think little more about it. However, do you ever notice that when we do get sick or hurt, then suddenly all of our attention and focus is on our illness like a laser beam? Nothing else matters at that time. We are strictly focused on our pain or illness. For these reasons, I place money after health in the grand scheme of things. The proper order of things in life, as per my Martian perspective is, time 1st, health 2nd, and money 3rd. The priority is time, health, and then money in that order. Let's move on to this 3rd priority now which includes the importance and respect of money.

Money

I place money and the respect for money as the 3rd priority. Time is the number one priority because we don't control or influence it and because we don't ever know precisely when our time is over. I guess that suicide would be an exception to this general rule. The concept of time is 1st priority in our earthly lives. You could die at any moment in an accident. You could die today crossing the street or shopping at the mall or driving to work or playing golf on a beautiful sunny day. It's a sobering thought and not pleasant to contemplate but what is...is! You can reduce your odds of dying by modifying your activities and behaviors, but lightning still strikes, freak storms and falling trees still occur.

Some authors suggest that we should live each day as if it is our last day on earth. That is a great idea because it forces us to respect the precious time that each of us does have. No amount of money can change the freak accident or storm that could end your life at any moment. In fact, if you have a lot of money and consequently are playing a lot of golf at your local club, you could increase your odds of dying due to a freak lightning storm due to just the frequency of playing the game. People could argue that a lot of money may prolong life but the quality and happiness of that life would likely suffer. To be healthy, energetic and full of life is truly magical. You can suddenly feel almost invincible, unstoppable and you really are. Your body can do work and your mind can solve problems and create win-win solutions. If our time is limited and uncontrollable, then it makes perfect sense to be as healthy and energetic as possible during our limited time on this planet.

Maintaining our health and vitality and ability to do work is therefore 2nd on the priority list. Many rich people will pay anything and sometimes everything to regain their precious health back. Money certainly helps in this instance but you don't need a lot of money to be healthy and happy. Money has its place to be sure and the respect of what your money can do is of utmost importance. What do I mean by respect of Your Money? Money is alive, if you will let it live. Money produces more money through interest payments, stock dividends, capital gains or mortgage interest or other cash-flow streams. Money makes the world go around. We certainly need SOME money to survive and thrive in our developed societies but just HOW MUCH we actually need is the tough question for many of us.

Almost all actions, trends and happenings in your neighborhood or in the world are related to money. Your spending choices have HUGE potential to alter markets and create new products or services. Where you spend your dollars can determine entire business trends. As a current example, the interest in health and wellness is driving the interest and investment in organic foods which then creates whole new businesses selling organic eggs, organic meats and organic fruits and vegetables. More and more organic foods are appearing on your grocery shelves because of the buying choices people are now making. The consumers are doing their talking with their dollars. If the existing companies don't listen, they will be left behind of the developing trend. The entire trend toward more organic foods is being driven by money choices made by consumers like YOU! If you are confused about a policy change or political event, just follow the flow of money and some answers may become quite clear.

As a real world example, our current world recession/correction can of course be traced back to money. Since 2008, our US economy and many other local and distant economies around the world have been negatively impacted by a basic lack of respect for money. Some experts on this topic suggest that the political goal to get every American into a home of their own was the initial cause. I agree. The process of buying a home usually involves saving up your money to create a suitable down payment. The down payment should obviously be as large as possible to show good faith and motivation on behalf of the home buyer. These down payments typically used to range between 10-20% of the house price. If you are buying a $100,000 house, you would need to come up with $10,000-$20,000 as a good faith down payment to complete the transaction.

The importance of that sizable down payment cannot be over stressed. The potential home buyers are showing a strong motivation to complete the deal which could run into decades of time with a 30 year mortgage etc. Now I understand that you will get less leverage with your money if you put a large down payment on your home, but you also get less risk of a default. This is your own home after all and it is not an investment property which produces cash-flow. Using maximum leverage for an investment property which generates positive cash-flow is another scenario completely. This investment property scenario, by the way, is an example of good debt where your invested monies are being used to create a positive monthly cash flow as well as an appreciating underlying asset. There really is good debt and bad debt. Unfortunately, most of us in the 99% are only familiar with bad debt such as car ownership, credit card balances, vacation loans, and other purchases of depreciating assets.

Good debt is involved with appreciating assets, such as real estate, rental homes and condominiums and maybe art and coin collections. Good debt can also create a positive monthly cash flow such as a rental property or business franchise purchase. Good debt should eventually create a positive monthly cash flow and the potential for a positive capital gain on the underlying asset that is purchased. When you borrow money to go into debt for a rental property that will generate free monthly cash and the potential for an increased value in the future, you are creating good debt. When you borrow money to go into debt for a personal use vehicle, you are not creating a positive monthly cash-flow and the vehicle is unlikely to increase in value (Blue Book Value) in the future. Your vehicle will be worth much less in 1-5 years and you have been making monthly payments all that time as well. If you were able to use that same vehicle in your own business and for business purposes, you would at least receive a tax break from the government for the use of this depreciating asset. I hope this explanation regarding good and bad debt helps to clarify the pros and cons of each type of financial obligation.

Your home is typically your largest initial investment. As you build up a solid base of assets, you may accumulate other properties and homes for strictly investment purposes. The political goal to put every American family into their own home does appear to be a good idea at first. But in this case, the devil was in the details of the home purchase. If you can buy a home with little or nothing down, what is your vested interest or what is your motivation to eventually complete the sale and own your home free and clear? In fact, the word Buy is not accurate in this case. You are really just renting or leasing or something else because so little of your monthly payments (mortgage?) are actually building equity in this most important asset of yours.

I assume most home buyers of this type were trying to get maximum leverage on their purchase using other people's money and then hoping the price of their home goes up magically forever to recoup all the interest and other charges. The whole process and political goal depended upon home prices rising steadily forever. This, of course, is not a realistic outcome. Now remember that the initial plan was to purchase your own home and possibly your biggest asset, something to own outright eventually. It was not meant to accumulate an investment property with positive cash-flow and price appreciation benefits.

By politically changing the rules of home buying, by reducing the down payment to little or nothing, we had created a monster. In a short period of time, the new highly-leveraged home buyers would be unable to meet their mortgage obligations and defaults would start occurring. The defaults would increase in numbers and soon the banks and mortgage companies and other home lenders would also be in trouble financially. And then due to globalization and some fancy new debt instruments, the home buying program that started in America would spread its financial woes throughout the developed world and that would lead us all into a global recession/depression that has been going on since 2008 or so. If you follow the money you can start to understand much larger and complicated social issues.

The housing crisis that originated in America and spread throughout the world was caused by a lack of respect for money. We tried to change the rules of buying a house to make it easier for first time home buyers. We wanted more people to purchase their own first home but at the same time, we forgot the rules of money. We also forgot the rules of growth. An asset like a house does not increase in price steadily year after year. There will normally be fluctuating economic cycles where the house price increases and decreases with some regularity. A larger down payment means a larger vested interest or motivation to complete the transaction in good faith regardless of temporary price fluctuations. A very small or no payment usually causes the opposite process to occur.

We have to understand money better. We have to become experts on the handling of money just like the elusive 1%. Excess money or savings equals choices/flexibility or a cushion to absorb life's little surprises. Living paycheck to paycheck is a very risky proposition and we can do much better. The odds are certainly against you if you choose to live paycheck to paycheck without a cash cushion to absorb life's little surprises. Feeling like a Martian among humans, I would watch as people worked hard for their weekly paycheck and then proceeded to spend most of it on superfluous luxuries and entertainment. This process would be repeated week after week, month after month, and year after year.

At the end of each year or during tax time, you could see exactly what you were paid and what you saved or invested. What is the purpose of work initially? At the beginning of your work career, I hope the purpose is to accumulate money and build up productive assets. Have you ever figured how much money has already gone thru your pockets? How much money have you actually earned already? Where is it? What happened to all of it? We are probably talking about thousands or tens of thousands of hard earned dollars already having gone thru your hands. Even if you have been working at minimum paying jobs, the total amount of money that has already passed through your hands will likely surprise you. That total money figure sure surprised this Martian when I performed my own calculation.

Hopefully, you will perform this calculation earlier in your work career then I did. The 1st five year working cycle is a great time to learn and implement this priceless information. The time that is lost, before you became aware of just how much money that you have already earned and spent, can never be replaced. Remember, time is the most precious commodity we have. What do you have to show for all your efforts? If that answer is nothing, then you need to change something.

As a Martian, I have tried and found this simple formula to work. I like to break up a lifetime in stages or five year cycles because this time frame seems to work well for many purposes. Other authors may use 10 year cycles or decades to study the changing environment as you go through your life. You can start the money accumulation process by putting in at least five years of steady hard work. During this 1st five year stage of work, you will concentrate solely upon accumulating/investing that money into your own new freedom/pension account. Learn to invest your savings as opposed to simply depositing those funds into a bank account. The banks can and do get rich on your free deposits otherwise. Do your own research and as of March 2017, you should be able to find 10% yields on some select investments such as REITS. Invest your hard earned monies in a brokerage account and find ETF's or REITS or other investment vehicles that pay approximately 10% yields. We will use the 10% yields as an example to keep the math simpler. You can make adjustments for your own portfolio if necessary.

We will assume a starting salary of $15,000. If you set aside at least 10% of your $15,000 salary, then you will have deposited approximately $1,500 into your 10% yielding investment account. If you do this, you will create a cash-flow or personal pension for yourself. Your $1,500 deposit in the investment account will actually generate 10% of $1,500 or $150 of free money every year for doing nothing. You get money for nothing and $150/year for free. You can enjoy and spend this income if you would like. You can spend some of this $150 and let the rest continue to grow larger or you can leave it alone and let the process really work well. You created the cash-flow by saving and investing intelligently in your own brokerage account.

For the first time in your life, you have created a positive cash-flow for yourself and your family. You have created a personal pension plan. Your newly created pension pays you every month or yearly forever and ever as long as you live and do not touch the invested nest egg. I am showing just the 1st five year cycle which could occur from age 25 to 30. Can you imagine what will happen to that monthly free gift as you continue thru three, four, of five more cycles. Does that sound exciting? Does that sound better than simply working, spending and consuming for 40 or more years until you are 65 and the government starts paying you a personal pension? And how much will you receive? Why risk it? You will still get whatever the government pension is when you retire. Hopefully however, the government pension will not be needed or will just become a bonus extra payment to supplement your own freedom pension.

There are whole books and even board games out there that describe the magic of positive cash-flow. In the previous example with $1,500 in investments and generating a yield of 10%, you would receive $150 yearly or approximately $12.50 monthly for doing nothing. Don't be too concerned about that small monthly amount in the beginning. That monthly gift will certainly grow larger with time, so just be patient and let the process continue for the full five years. The invested money will finally start working for you instead of you working for the money. Instead of working your whole life for money, these simple changes would make your money work for you.

Now let's carry this scenario for five years of work and watch what happens to the magic of cash flow. Assuming no increases in pay, in five years you would have earned 5 x $15,000 = $75,000. I am deliberately using a low average yearly salary to show that everyone can do this. You just have to start somewhere and let the magic of regular long- term investing work for you.

You would have invested at least $1,500/year x 5 years = $7,500 at 10% yield. This five year effort would have created your own freedom pension containing at least $7,500 @ 10% yield = $750 yearly or approximately $65 monthly for doing no work. Your money is now really working for you. Of course, you can increase these numbers dramatically by earning more and investing more. The growth of the invested money would be at least doubled if you had a life partner/spouse to work with.

I have read that Asian cultures typically save 20-30% and more of their income. As mentioned earlier, if you have a life partner or spouse, then all the numbers are doubled again. Once you see the process in action, it is hard not to make a game of it. Chart your results and place them on the refrigerator door. Chart your results on a large poster and place it where you and your family will see it every day. Have monthly finance meetings with your family. Watch your financial position get stronger month by month and year over year for the first five years of steady, hard work and dedicated regular investment. Involve your child or children in the process. Make it fun and spend some of the monthly cash flow on something special. Make it a life-long habit of regular cash deposits into your investment account.

What is the main purpose of work for you? If you work just to spend it all, what do you expect to have at the end? You will probably have a lot of stuff, a lot of debt, and a lot of stress but not a lot of choices or freedom. Let's play with some more five year numbers now. As a Martian, I believe that a working couple can create a sizable cash flow in a five year period. This cash flow or personal freedom pension will continue to generate monthly income forever if you allow it. The pension and cash flow is alive, it is generating offspring (dividends and capital gains) and you just have to care for it. It is like a golden goose that lays golden eggs as long as you take care of it. Don't kill the goose! Don't touch that invested nest egg.

If your life partner and yourself are earning $20,000 each annually, then in five years the two of you will have earned $40,000 x 5 = $200,000. That's a lot of money from average paying jobs. Instead of just saving 10%, our hypothetical couple saves 30% of their income (they want freedom faster than most). 30% of their combined annual income = 30% of $40,000 which equals (0.30 x $40,000) = $12,000 savings annually. Now five years of this cycle = 5 x $12,000= $60,000 in savings/investments. That's $60,000 in investments that is alive and generating income. In just five years of time, you and your life partner have created a golden nest egg of $60,000 @ 10% yield =$6,000 annually or $500 monthly.

You and your partner/spouse have just created a lifetime pension that is currently generating $500 a month. That's a lot of free money that you didn't have to work for. You will have $500 every month or $6,000 every year from that time onward. That personal pension was created by working and investing diligently for just five years. This couple could have started their five year cycle at 25 years of age. Here they are, at just 30 years old, with a monthly positive cash flow of $500. There was probably little fun to be had during this 1st five year time period and lots of working but the payoff is well worth the effort involved. The payoff continues for the rest of your life and beyond if you desire.

I believe that any working couple can basically retire in five years or at least create a lot of options/choices/flexibility in their financial futures. You could eliminate all debt and have a monthly allowance of $500 forever. Suddenly, you have options with your financial future. You have flexibility and a cash cushion to help you and yours into the future. You can work part-time or start your own business, or start a family. If you work hard and steady for five years and invest your substantial savings at a good yield, you will have created a monthly cash cushion that allows choices, flexibility and power.

When you hear of old money or trust accounts for children, this is evidence of the magical power of compounding interest and cash flow over a long period of time. Imagine this five year process continuing for 20, 30, 50, or more years as your children and grandchildren continue to regularly invest and never touch the constantly growing golden nest egg. What would you be like with $500 monthly coming in for free? What is your stress level for the future? What choices do you have now? You could work part time. You could start your own business. You could slow down and think more.

As a Martian, I believe strongly in living FAR BELOW your financial means particularly in the early five year work cycles. Concentrate on investing regularly and building your golden nest egg. Work, eat, sleep, and invest because the future payoff will amaze you. Your creative problem-solving computer will find ways to live well on less and then you avoid a lot of stress, sickness and complications. I did say that you can learn to live WELL on LESS! That was not a typo error. You can thrive on less money and not just survive. Other humans have done this before you and they had a super creative computer just like yours. If they managed to do it then why can't you? Start respecting your money. Don't waste your money. Think of every financial transaction you undertake each day. Is this transaction respecting my money? Am I getting good value for my money? Am I buying something unnecessary?

Your spending choices have significant potential to alter entire markets as well. Where you spend your dollars will determine business trends. The current interest in health and well- being is an example. The health and well-being trend is creating a stronger interest in organic foods which can lead to new operations selling organic eggs, organic meals, and organic fruits and vegetables. More and more organic foods are appearing on your grocery shelves because of the buying choices people are now making. The entire trend towards more organic foods is being driven by money choices made by consumers.

Always remember to watch the flow of money when you are trying to understand a new trend in our society. Money makes this world go round. If a large successful corporation does something to displease its customers and those customers make a choice to spend their money elsewhere, that corporation will have to make quick changes or face possible bankruptcy. Where you spend your money is so important to future trends on this planet. We can make good buying choices that help us and our planet or bad ones. We have the power and we have the choice.

If you insist upon unlimited, expensive entertainment to escape your current reality, then the marketplace will provide it. And our society will continue to create highly paid musicians, sports figures, corporate CEO's, hedge fund managers etc. etc. If we insist on drugs such as heroin, cocaine, or pain killers to escape our current realities, then the market place will provide them. If you have customers with cash in their pockets, the products will be created to satisfy this demand. Just follow the money.

Think about where your money is being spent and what new markets are being created to satisfy you. Use that incredible creative problem solving computer on your shoulders to come up with a better way. You can do better. We can all do better. A lot of money experts suggest you save or invest at least 10% of your income. If you earn $20,000 annually then at the end of the calendar year, you should have at least $2,000 put away or invested for a rainy day. As you read and study and learn more about money you will discover how money is alive. It wants to expand and produce other monies. Money will start to work for you when you invest as opposed to just depositing your earnings in a bank or other savings institution.

What do you think happens to the money you deposit in a bank? What does the bank do with your money? Nowadays, most banks will give a small amount of interest for the use of your money but the percentages are very low and certainly will not prove profitable for the depositors. Do you think that is all that happens with your money at the bank? Perhaps you have heard that the banks invest

YOUR money and earn good returns from YOUR hard earned cash. Of course, this is true! How do you think the banks have become so powerful and wealthy? Free money that is invested intelligently can become a mountain of dollars over time. Guess what? The banks are experts at investing money. You can become an expert at investing money.

Warren Buffett, George Soros, and Bill Gates are all experts at investing money. Why can't you and I do it as well? I bet you already know the answer! They are just human with that same brain and body thing we keep hearing about.

The BIG difference is that they respect their money and what that money can accomplish if properly cared for. Do you currently respect your money? Most people will tell you that you have to work to pay your bills. Most people tell you that you will be working for around 40 years from say 25 to 65 years of age. Hopefully at age 65, your working life is done. Who makes these work rules? Are we really put on this planet with our incredible gifts of body and brains to work the best years of our lives doing something monotonous, repetitive and soul destroying? Are we expected to use all of our magnificent equipment to do menial and simplistic jobs which are usually designed to make someone else rich? Is our main purpose in this precious life to work endlessly in order to get money to buy needless stuff and expensive, continuous, sedentary entertainment?

Do you see the problem here? You work and then spend most of your earnings on more and more STUFF and/or entertainment. I read recently that the savings rate for Americans under age 35 is actually negative. This means that the group as a whole is going into debt and actually reducing their net worth each year. This behaviour will likely guarantee that you must keep on working until a monthly government pension finally takes over and provides a positive cash-flow.

If your spending was reduced, you would break this insane working cycle. You would then start to build a cash cushion or buffer to protect you and yours from life's little financial surprises. You would create a freedom account for yourself and your family as needed. These savings are crucial for your financial future. These savings give you flexibility, choices, control, and power over your destiny. If you work for a year and earn $15,000 for your efforts and actually set aside 10% of those wages ($1,500), you will have accomplished something very important. You know that the year is gone and you are one year older, but you don't know if the job will continue unchanged next year. If you are able to work at that same job for five years and have earned (5 x $15,000) = $75,000, and you have set aside at least $7,500 (10%) in your freedom account, then you have just created something powerful and tangible.

What would you have if you spent all your earnings instead? What would be left after five years of hard work and lost time? You would have nothing to show for all your efforts. You would be five years older for sure and that same job may be gone forever or changed drastically. Some people may actually be in more bad debt than when they started out working five years ago. Can you imagine working hard for five years and actually being worse off financially speaking? You could have done nothing for those same five years and come out ahead. You could have laid out on the beach, gone fishing, watched TV, or just vegged out for all those years and you would be better off net-worth wise. Is that not INSANE behaviour? Surely we can do better.

If you don't save regularly and set aside some of your precious earnings each and every year into your own pension, then you will likely have to work until a government or employer pension kicks in for you. You can become an expert on money, savings, investments, and monthly cash flow. Use that new money expertise to create more free time for yourself by building a cash cushion. Give yourself maximum job flexibility and choices. Use your new money skills to work less but earn more.

The whole process usually begins with the creation of a cash cushion or money buffer to allow you time and space to think creatively. Slow the pace of your current life down so you can relax and think more on your current challenges. Maybe now you can consider part time work or starting your own business. Work hard and save hard and then invest hard for five years to create that cash buffer. Then slow down and think about the next five year cycle.

Can you reduce your hours at work via part time employment or freelance consulting? Can you work from your home and simplify things? A five year time frame is a useful way to section off your life. You work hard and full time for the 1st five year cycle, then maybe part time or creating your own employment for the 2nd five years. Your part time work may even allow another person to get a financial start of their own by creating another part-time job from a previously full-time position. Each new five year cycle is better for you and yours financially. You will be working on your terms for a change. You will be working on your schedule and under your control for a change.

This control of your financial life will no doubt reduce your stress level and thereby increase your health. You will have a quiet, unpretentious power within yourself. You are finally starting to respect your magnificent body and brain and its amazing capabilities. Your confidence, self- esteem, and personal power will continue to grow in an upward spiral of awareness and enlightenment. Eventually, the monthly cash flow created by your working efforts will cover all expenses and even leave some extra fun monies to play with. I think we humans call that point in our lives, retirement.

If you don't improve financially each year and increase your net worth annually, then what is the purpose of working at all? We all have limited working years in our lives and we have to make them count. All of us humans are here for a very short time and we never even know when our lives can be ended due to accidents, sickness, or disease. We do not and cannot control time on this planet. How can we spend the best 30 or 40 or more years of our precious lives working at jobs that we dislike and can't control? We waste a lot of our years being frustrated, angry, and sad because we THINK we must always be working to pay our monthly bills. Why do we think this way? Have you ever heard or thought about consumerism? Have you ever heard or thought about advertisers and marketers of an endless supply of products? But who actually controls these monthly bills? Who controls the monthly expenses that reduce or eliminate our magic cash flow? WE DO.

You may have noticed how everyone wants a piece of your income stream/cash-flow. There are car payments, telephone and utility payments, cable/satellite contracts, lawn maintenance contracts, computer, security service, cell phone, you name it monthly payments that the vendors just love to set up for you. These vendors know the importance of positive monthly cash-flow for their own bottom lines. When you want to set up another service, the vendors will study your existing cash-flow to see if there is any extra money available. If these providers have their way, most or all of your monthly cash-flow will be directed or flowed to them.

You might earn $1,000 a month but $1,000 also goes out every month. You might earn $2,000, $3,000, $5,000 monthly but it doesn't matter because most or all of that monthly cash-flow is still probably flowing out. There is no lack of sellers who want a piece of your monthly cash-flow. You have to protect your hard earned monthly cash-flow.

Ask yourself every payday if you are putting some money aside for you and your family. Are you balancing your earnings with your savings or investments? Have you become unbalanced in your financial affairs with regular earnings but no regular investments? As a new reader of financial materials, you will likely come across the phrase: "pay yourself first" as a general rule to achieve freedom from the wage slave cycle. This general rule or concept involves always taking a portion of your earnings (at least 10%) and investing these monies for your financial future. Before you pay all those other service providers, you pay yourself and be the first in line. If you just got paid $500.00, then you would take out $50.00 or $100.00 or $150.00 and invest it in your personal pension. Pay yourself first for all your troubles/efforts. If you spend it all without saving anything, then you will likely be working for a long time and hoping and praying for those golden retirement years.

We need some money to function effectively on this planet. How much money we actually need to just survive and then to thrive is a good question. The question is an individual one that we can eventually answer, I hope. At what point in your working life would you like to accumulate this needed nest egg and the cash-flow that comes with it? It makes good sense to my Martian mind to get the initial nest egg quickly out of the way while you are healthy, energetic, and strong. The 1st five years of your working career seems to be the logical choice because you will then have your whole life to enjoy the free cash-flow. The 1st five years could be from age 20 to 25 or from age 25 to 30 depending upon when you started receiving regular income from an employer.

If you are currently in your later working years, then you should be more aggressive in your savings/investment rate (30% or greater) to help make up for lost time. Whatever your age is (at the starting point for the creation of the investment nest egg), the key is to proceed quickly and respect your precious time on this planet. You can start thinking in terms of five year cycles of earning and investing money. A five year time frame works pretty well considering how quickly things are changing in the business world. If you have the same job and same pay/responsibilities at the same company after five years, you are doing well. The concept of a 20 or 30 year career at a single company is becoming a rare commodity nowadays.

Did you notice the word unbalanced in the previous section? We will now discuss how balance or moderation in all things can be incorporated in our lives. Time, health, and money are the proper order of things in my Martian world. Now we will see how a balanced approach to these three concepts is ideal.

TO SUM UP:

In my Martian world or way of thinking, you would:

Put the concept of money in 3rd place in our human life priorities after time and health. No matter how much money you may have accumulated, there isn't much you can do with that money to buy your health back in most cases.

Balance your pursuit of money while still respecting the importance of your health and your limited and unknown amount of time on this planet. Because we never know when our time is up, a person could die at a young age and never get to enjoy the nest egg that was created.

Put the odds in your favor of a good future financial outcome by quickly creating an investment nest egg that pays out monthly dividends etc.

Create your personal pension early in your working career (1st five year cycle) such as from age 25 to 30 and make the best use of your limited money earning/working years.

Save and invest more aggressively (30% to 50% or more) if you are in the later years of your working career. The quicker the nest egg is created and producing cash-flow, the better.

Become more aware of and protect your positive cash-flow from unnecessary monthly charges.

Increase your cash-flow month by month and year by year and track your progress with a chart or other visual aid to make things more interesting and fun.

CHAPTER 4: BALANCE OR MODERATION IN ALL THINGS

After you have reorganized your life priorities, the next level of information and insight comes from balance. There should be balance or moderation in all areas of our lives. I'm quite sure that you have met someone who seems to do everything in extremes. If they are a jogger for instance, then they are running all the time. They run every day for so many miles or so many hours at the expense of other areas in their lives. Their social, financial, educational, family, spiritual areas can be neglected due to the unbalanced pursuit of jogging. The key word is unbalanced.

In one sense, the dedication and determination to pursue jogging is admirable but not at the expense of the other important qualities. Of course, jogging and fitness are important but so are the other facets of our worlds. We have to use our extensive creative powers to find a workable solution to this challenge. If all you do in your spare time is to jog, then what happens to your close relationships, your life goals, your mental development, your creative faculties, and your future financial plans? We only have so many hours in our days to accomplish so much. We need to balance our efforts in all important areas to get the best overall result. We need to balance our efforts to put the odds in our favor of a good future outcome.

If you are running every spare moment you have, for instance, and always training for the next major/minor competition, there is a good chance that you are neglecting other areas in your life. You would also increase the odds of getting injured in your unbalanced pursuit of running. At that point, you may have damaged your health while actually trying to improve your fitness level. Obviously, some running or aerobic exercise is useful for a healthy body but always in balance and moderation.

Some self-help reading is helpful, some recreational reading is good, some time spent earning money and building net worth is great but all these things should be part of a balanced total life style. It is always a question of balance. If you are currently doing something out of balance with your other life goals, then become aware of the problem and make necessary changes. You had a long run on Monday, then take Tuesday off and do some reading or relationship work with your spouse or family members. Spend at least ½ hour each day doing something physical and ½ hour reading something uplifting or inspirational.

Always strive for a balance in the main areas of life. Simply split your daily time doing something physical, mental, social, spiritual, nutritional, financial, and don't forget fun. Do not focus on one specific area at the expense of the others. You may turn out to be a great runner, but at a high cost to your other life priorities. You may actually harm your health in your unbalanced pursuit of health. It seems quite easy to become focused on just one or two areas of your life, so simple AWARENESS of the condition is important.

Just watch how you spend your waking hours and keep track mentally or take notes daily. Before you retire to bed, replay the day that you just had and just become aware of the good and bad points over the last 24 hours. What changes would you like to make if it was possible to replay that day? How could you modify things to make it mostly good or great? Tomorrow is a brand new day to try out something different. Did you get a little exercise or have a vigorous work out today? How many self-help/ inspirational books have you read this past month? Just by becoming highly aware of how you use your precious daily time will be very beneficial for fine tuning the activities in your life.

Some people have highly developed bodies but poorly developed minds. They exercise a great deal but they do not read enough. Or the opposite is also possible where a well-read person has neglected his/her physical body. These humans read a lot but find little or no time for exercise. Many experts on the topic suggest that we all require three simple things to function at our best for as long as possible. Those three things include: adequate nutrition via diet, adequate physical exercise via cardio and strength training, and stress management. It all comes down to three main things to do to put the odds in your favor for a long and healthy life. Once those three items are individually taken care of, we can concentrate on the others.

Become aware of how your days are being used. Where are you spending your waking time? Try doing an hour by hour mental replay of yesterday as you drift off to sleep. Are you balanced in your efforts? Are you neglecting your social responsibilities? Are you spending enough time on your important personal relationships? You have probably seen or heard of a father who is solely focused on earning money for his family but is rarely even available to interact with that family. The man thinks that he is doing the right thing by trying to provide for all his family needs. If he is asked why so much time is spent working so long and hard, he may say that he is doing it all for his wife and children.

Once again, working hard is admirable when it is a balanced activity. The man may become rich and successful but be divorced and estranged from his children. He may become rich and successful and yet have a shortened life-span due to high stress, poor nutrition, and lack of adequate exercise. The man in this case needs to look out for himself primarily. That statement may sound selfish at first, but if he does not take care of himself, who will or who is expected to? If he becomes very sick or dies, what happens to all of his dependants? Ultimately, we all have to look out for ourselves to increase the odds of a favorable outcome. In my Martian opinion, we have to take care of ourselves first and then we can CHOOSE to take care of others.

It always seems to come down to the odds of something occurring. Put the odds in your favor. Use your creative ability and physical skill to influence the outcome of your life. Why leave things up to chance when you can exert some control or influence on your life's outcome? Working hard and jogging hard are both admirable qualities but only as a balanced part of a whole life. Your family may have all of their financial needs met but at the expense of a close connection between you and them. Naturally, this scenario can also occur with the hard driving professional female who has decided that she wants it all. She works a full day at the office and then starts a second shift at home with her spouse and children. It would be like working a 16 hour day plus commuting time. The levels of stress in her life must be considerable and usually the people around our hard working lady will also suffer as a result.

Once again, the working, hard driving, determination is a good quality but only if it is part of a whole balanced life. So how on earth can we work less to have more time in our busy, complicated lives? In my Martian opinion, the answer is to reduce your current cash expenditures and live far below your financial means. You can also learn how to earn more money doing less hours of work. Start using your creative, problem solving computer and focus on this challenge. If you simplify your life and thus reduce your monthly bills, you will need less money to get by and still be happy. You will learn to live well on less just like other humans have already done.

Start the process by drawing up a monthly budget to see exactly where your money is being spent. Be brutally honest with yourself when you are preparing this document. Where do you currently spend all of your money? Where does it all go each month or each year? You worked long and hard to earn this cash, so why not work long and hard to carefully spend it? Put in the effort to learn to respect this money and learn to invest it to make it grow forever. Are you getting good value for your spending? Are you just accumulating more stuff so you have the most at the end? By carefully spending your weekly earnings for a change, you will not have to work as many hours for the same or better lifestyle. You will start to learn to live WELL on LESS.

This exercise will free up some precious time to re-balance your total life picture. Are you and yours worth the effort? Most people recoil at the thought of doing a budget but how else can you get an accurate picture of your current spending? Most, if not all, small and large businesses, entire corporations, and world- wide conglomerates work with a budget. These business entities are experts with their spending and investing. We have to become experts with our family spending and investing as well. We dislike writing up a budget because we expect that painful financial choices will then have to be made and we are probably correct in this assumption. If you are constantly lacking money, always in debt, always having to work, and your net worth is still decreasing every year, then you need help with your finances and monthly budget. The help that you need will now hopefully come from your own reading and research.

Your completed monthly budget will finally show the problems in your spending habits. Re-balance your spending so you can still have some fun, some entertainment, but also some savings, some investments, some financial flexibility. You can create a cash cushion to soften the inevitable bumps in life. When you spend most of your earnings on expensive entertainment or eating out at restaurants, then you will probably have nothing but memories of a good time or a full belly at the end of the tax year. You will certainly be a year older, your job may change for the worse, your job may disappear, and your weekly pay may decrease even though your job responsibilities may increase. Everything is constantly changing in this life all the time. Death, taxes, and continuous change are a certainty in our world.

Learn to balance your spending habits with your new saving habits. Learn to live well on less and to re-appreciate the simpler things in life such as a quiet, thoughtful conversation with your partner or close friend, spending quality time with your family, taking a long walk with your dog, watching a sunrise or sunset, etc. etc. Pretty much every time that you purchase something, you will complicate your life and reduce your precious free time. Give these new purchases a lot of consideration. Are they truly worth the extra complications and reduced free time? Are you just adding a distraction or time- waster to your routine?

Most things that you purchase require maintenance, storage, and upkeep. Sometimes when we move from house to house, we transport boxes of stuff that were never opened or even used at the old house. Public storage facilities seem to be a growing business because of this behavior. Repacking boxes full of stuff that was never used in the past couple of years is not a good use of your time. This old stuff will now travel to your new location for more storage. You probably purchased a larger home for just such a purpose.

Remember that you are working hard to keep this insanity going. More and more stuff to take care of, more complications, more time wasters and an unbalanced life. Our homes continue to get larger, our closets and storage spaces continue to expand and yet most of us are overflowing with depreciating assets. If you can't take all this stuff with you at death, then shouldn't we be reducing as we age and not collecting more and more of these time wasters that complicate our lives.

Your completed budget will reveal any problems in black and white numbers. Learn to balance your absolute needs with your ever changing desires. Recycle and repair what you already have until something new is really, truly needed and then throw out the old or donate if possible so as not to add more things to your life. As we get older and wiser, we should be reducing our stuff and simplifying our lives for our survivors. You cannot take it with you. Make an effort to reduce your stuff, reduce these time wasters, reduce your maintenance duties, simplify your life, and take back some precious time for your existence. You can do it. I did it. Other people have done it.

Use that magnificent body and creative, problem solving brain of yours to find a better way. You are magnificent. You can do better. Study, watch, and make adjustments to your own world to create more time, less stress, more health, and more choices and flexibility. Become constantly AWARE of how your time is being spent and readjust to equalize all areas of life.

As a Martian, I try to enjoy all aspects of life on a daily basis. Everyday a little exercise, a little productive reading, a little recreational reading or listening to CD stories, a little family time, a little eating, and, of course, a little relaxation time and fun. You can build structure into your daily activities but life has to be fun as well. You must ultimately create a life that makes you happy most of the time. There will always be sad times or hard times in this life because you cannot win all the time. As a basic condition of human life, you will win some but you will also lose some.

By keeping yourself happy most of the time, you can balance out the inevitable down times. Learn to create your own customized life by using your incredible body and mind. You want a life that makes you mostly happy, mostly unstressed, and mostly healthy. You will then put the odds in your favor as you deal with life's challenges. That's about all you can do, in my Martian opinion, to increase the number of good outcomes in our lives. There is rarely a black or white answer in human affairs and rarely a guarantee of something happening.

Balancing the work cycle with the re-creation (recreation) cycle is possible. Start creating more free time in your daily schedule to think more, to reflect more, and to readjust your life priorities and fine tune your new life. Surely we were not given these magnificent tools of body and mind just to work our prime years doing something mundane, repetitive, and soul destroying for somebody else. Forty years of precious, prime time doing something that you dislike, 40 years under the control of someone else, 40 years of outside stress because you don't control your own work cycle. Is this what human life is all about? Is our main purpose in life to try and find a good job and then work 9 to 5 Monday to Friday for 50 weeks every year for at least 40 years? I certainly don't think so but, apparently, a lot of other humans do based upon what is seen in the developed countries.

How do you start the process of exiting this rat race/work cycle? How do you retake control of your life work cycle? My simple answer is to start building personal savings now. We humans need some money to function effectively in our world. If we neglect to get that money cushion or life buffer then even our health may start to suffer as we can be forced to work at jobs that are harming us. Give yourself and your family some financial breathing room. Many money experts suggest keeping 3 to 6 months of basic living expenses in a liquid investment account. These savings will lead to personal investments which will lead to a personal pension/cash flow which will eventually lead to your own control, your own choices and flexibility in regards to your working career.

Finally, you are in control, you are at the wheel and you are the captain of your ship. Always try to balance your earnings with your spending habits. For every dollar earned, you would save a dollar at least in theory. That would be a 50% savings rate which, of course, is possible but tough to put into practice. At a 50% savings rate on your take home pay, that five year process of building personal savings would really take off and your exit from the rat race would be fast tracked.

Your savings rate on your take home pay is your choice of course. Just remember that the more you save EARLY in your working career, the more you will eventually have and the faster you will take control of your work cycle. Nowadays, everything is about speed and getting things quickly. You get a brand new car on credit just after you get your driving license or you move into a new fully furnished home on credit just after you are married. There seems to be little waiting or planning for these major life events. I want it now whatever the cost or complication.

Interestingly, a classic sign of maturity is delayed gratification. It is more mature to delay your accumulation of depreciating assets or general stuff until you are better prepared financially. If you buy a car that retails for $20,000 dollars but you only actually give the car dealer a token $1,000 dollars down payment to drive the car away, then did you actually BUY the car? Are you just using it and paying a monthly fee to do so? You never really own it until many years later when you may finally receive the car title free and clear and you no longer have to send those monthly car payments to your bank or finance company.

If you had delayed your gratification to have a car for even a year or two, then you could accumulate a larger down payment and have smaller monthly charges to your cash flow. Or, you could buy a good used car for cash with no more monthly payments at all. I bet you can figure out my own choice. You would actually own the used car outright in this example and your precious monthly cash flow would not be affected. The new car that you are paying a monthly fee to drive would not be actually owned by you until the end of the finance contract. You are really just paying a monthly fee to borrow the new car and it is depreciating in value every day as well.

This is a good example of not respecting your hard earned money. Do you really need the new car NOW? Do you really need a NEW car at all? Could you borrow a car instead from your family or friends and pay them for the privilege? This scenario might actually help them and help you at the same time. Could you rent a car from a dealer only during those times when it is actually needed? There is a lot of information out there concerning the very high cost of owning a car. Even the IRS will currently allow you a deduction of over 0.50 cents per mile to use your vehicle for business purposes. If you drive 20 miles back and forth to work, then it has cost you at least (20 miles x 0.50) = $10. That $10 trip to work includes gas, oil, taxes, licensing, depreciation, financing, lease payments, wear and tear, etc. etc. Find this information out for yourself and carefully read it, study it, and finally implement some changes in your car ownership world if possible. I am sure that you will be shocked at the numbers involved because they certainly surprised me.

Learn to balance your accumulation of depreciating assets with the appropriate amount of time to fully pay for those purchases. This balancing act will reduce your debt load and outgoing cash flow and your overall stress level. Learn to balance your outflow of money or purchases to your inflow of money or earnings. Let your earnings growth rate and investment cushion decide how quickly that you start to accumulate assets. Delay your gratification and be more mature when considering large purchases. The larger the purchase, then the more time spent thinking and analyzing the decision. Slow down and give yourself time to consider the pros and cons of the purchase. Do you really need this item now? Can you come up with a better or more creative alternative?

Impulse buying is usually a bad idea and store owners regularly exploit this behaviour with impulse racks located conveniently at check outs. Give yourself the time and respect that these major purchases deserve. Balance in life is just one of those concepts that appears too easily to work and yet, of course, it does. I have found in my life that the easiest and most elegant solution is probably the best. Apply moderation in all things including food intake, exercise, free time, work time, and even earning money. If you eat too much, you will suffer. If you eat too little, you will suffer. Find the balance and moderate your intake of food to provide just enough food for good nutrition, ideal body weight, and subsequently good health. Too much exercise can be detrimental to your body while too little exercise can result in a number of physical and mental problems.

There is so much out there in the world to experience. A little taste of a lot of different things is better than concentrating all of your efforts on just a few items or areas of life. Every new day, try doing a little reading to learn something new or inspirational, some moderate or vigorous exercise, some family, friend, or pet time, have some fun time and stay mostly happy. Feel free to experiment and find the balance point for all of your areas of life. If you only concentrate on earning money and you become a workaholic with no other hobbies, friends, or interests outside of work, then your other life compartments will suffer as a result.

The familiar story of the man or woman working all of the time to try and provide everything that their family desires is a good example of unbalanced effort. These over worked people rarely have the time or energy to nurture and build the relationships between themselves and their beneficiaries. The over worked person can become a stranger in their own family. Of course, if there is no family involved, then the only one to suffer from the unbalanced work effort will be the individual involved. If a father rarely takes the time to play and interact with his son or daughter and he misses important events such as graduation, 1st prom, 1st date, then he will likely become a stranger to his own children.

The children will grow up whether we are ready or not to finally take more interest in them. This chunk of time cannot be slowed down or stopped or replayed again. It is gone forever and the children are now adults. If you are unbalanced with the work component of your life, then you will likely lose these precious moments in your child's life. You will have memories and even pictures of these past events, but it is not possible to go back in time and replay the years. Always remember the ultimate importance of time. It is time, health, and then money in that order in my Martian opinion.

Our current society encourages unbalanced behaviour such as over working, over eating, or over spending. Many books, movies, and advertisements promote the hard driving, money at all costs, workaholic who will stop at nothing to get MORE. How much is enough you ask? The answer is MORE! Why are there so many books, movies, etc. promoting unbalanced behaviour? Is it just plain entertainment or something else? Naturally, most advertisements are designed to sell or market a product. The advertisers would like you to continue buying their product or service whether you really need it or not. You don't tend to see many ads showing a person eating a nutrient dense wholesome meal of adequate proportions in a relaxed setting. I guess that picture would not sell much product.

Unbalanced behaviors in the media are everywhere and maybe that explains a lot of the insane activity out there. In many cases, the object of the game of life is to accumulate the largest pile of stuff before you die. Whoever has the most at the end is the winner. Hopefully this discussion on balance in all areas of life and moderation in all things will provide some guidance and information to help you fine tune your own little world for the better. We will next have to become familiar with a very powerful, but sneaky influence on our decisions, behaviors and entire lives. I call it ego.

TO SUM UP:

In my Martian world or way of thinking, you would:

Start the process of balancing your daily time and effort in the six or so major areas of human life.

Try to spend equal amounts of time and attention in your social, financial, nutritional, educational, spiritual, and physical areas of life.

Do not pursue just one area of a complete life at the expense of the others.

Don't become a fitness addict who chooses not to read or study something educational on a daily basis.

Don't become a fitness addict who has little time for family and friends.

Don't become a book worm or intellectual who neglects their physical body and nutritional needs.

For balanced health in general, start reading and researching on adequate daily nutrition (vitamins and minerals) via diet, adequate daily physical exercise via cardio and strength training, and stress management and reduction.

During your initial working career or my Martian 1st five year work cycle, I put much more emphasis on accumulating a nest egg and creating a monthly cash flow.

Build up that golden nest egg and start receiving some free monthly golden eggs as early as possible and as quickly as possible in your working life.

Become more mature and delay your gratification for more and more stuff/depreciating assets.

There is so much to explore and experience on this planet that we don't want to focus on only one aspect of human life at the expense of others. Try and get a little taste of everything possible.

Become a generalist on many topics/things instead of a specialist in a few select areas with the following exceptions.

Become an expert/specialist with your limited time on earth, your daily health status, and your finances.

CHAPTER 5: THE ELUSIVE AND POWERFUL EGO

In my Martian opinion, much of our suffering and struggle seen and endured on this planet is caused/ influenced by our EGOS. Some authors suggest that all of our suffering on planet earth is ego related. The point is that our egos are a major influence on our day to day lives and our hour to hour decisions. The ego is that powerful and yet who even gives it a second thought? Most or all of our suffering on this planet is directly related to our very own egos. When your ego gets involved in any discussion, transaction, or just plain interaction with another human being, trouble usually follows. In all of my self-help research to date, I still don't know what our egos are good for. They do help us stand out from the crowd and become separate entities but at what cost? Is there a good purpose for our egos?

This question continues to fascinate and interest me. I am very aware of all the trouble that the ego can get us into but there must be a good reason for it to be so influential in our existence. Perhaps we must suffer on a daily basis in order to burn up the ego. When the ego is finally burned up through suffering, humans could then move up to another level of existence. This new elevated position would create a far better and less insane planet. Maybe we are in the process of suffering through the ego to move on and up towards a more enlightened awareness. It is almost like we humans have a built in self-destruct mechanism for some unknown reason.

Just becoming AWARE of our ego and how it directs so much of our behavior is a crucial 1st step in our awakening process. When you start to watch it operate, usually just below the surface of our many day to day interactions, it is an enlightening and scary exercise. I feel that the greatest thing we can do as a species in the future is to reduce our ego's power/influence and work towards becoming EGOLESS in our daily lives. Just seeing the word egoless in a book, on your refrigerator, or written across your bathroom mirror, can be a gentle reminder to stay aware of its everyday existence.

To operate in an egoless state most of the time would definitely reduce the human suffering and conflict that is so prevalent in our current reality. Reducing our ego's influence and operating more from an egoless point of view would eliminate much of the useless conflict between people, countries, nations, religions, etc. Your ego is normally involved in just about every decision both large and small that you make daily. What you wear, what you eat, what you drive to work, what you do on weekends, what you do on holidays, etc. etc. are all probably driven and decided by our egos.

The clothes that you wear to work were always interesting to me in my early working career. Unless the company insists on a very specific uniform, then shouldn't the employees be able to wear comfortable, inexpensive, yet professional looking clothes? If certain clothes must be worn according to your employer, do they need to be so costly and name brand? Is there a less expensive alternative that would suffice? I would be afraid to guess what the monthly work clothing budget is for many jobs. What do the latest fashion trends even mean? Why do they change with such regularity? Could there be a money motive behind all of this? You could own a suit that went out of fashion years ago, according to the fashion experts, only to discover that now it is alright to wear it again. Who makes these rules and what do they even mean? Could there be a money component behind these societal rules?

Some person or fashion company dictates a new fashion trend that is often just a repeat of years gone by. What is really wrong with your older clothing at the moment? Remember to follow the money when you are confused about a new trend or process. A new fashion trend would drive additional sales for the clothing being advertised. You as a consumer would be out of fashion if you did not immediately go out and purchase this newly created proper clothing. I wonder what the price and quality of this new fashion is compared to the old one. What happens if you are out of current fashion? Are there fashion police out there to enforce this clothing trend?

Your purchasing decisions are being created or influenced by an elusive and ever changing body of fashion designers. They are experts in this field. You know what that means. You will have to become and expert to properly counter their expert selling techniques. The fashion designers would very much like you to purchase their new, fashionable garments and your ego will probably agree with them. Who doesn't want to own the latest and newest fashion? Your ego probably feels that the new outfit will make you a better and more successful person. You want to fit in and follow the crowd. What happens if you don't buy them quickly before they are out of fashion again? It seems that we are back to the unbalanced accumulation of more stuff to sooth our ego's needs once again.

Yearly changes in car designs, appliances, home furnishings, computers, cell phones, almost everything possible drives our egos to make new purchases whether actually needed or not. If the manufacturers want to sell more products, then they just have to change the design, color, size, cost, or whatever and the 99% will do their best to purchase the new items. This process is an ongoing and powerful influence that attempts to create endless consumers of all of us. I understand that our current economy is based upon endless and ongoing consumption. But in my Martian world, maybe we can shift some of those dollars into other things like planet pollution, species extinction, environmental toxins and new man-made chemicals, climate change, deforestation, creating a BETTER world for our children and grandchildren. We could certainly reduce our endless consumption of EGO needs and transfer those monies into EARTH needs. We are always buying something new and in fashion and hopefully improved. We are always trying to keep up with our neighbors, coworkers, family, or relatives.

If our neighbor buys the latest model of car, then we must have it as well. Even though your current vehicle is doing just fine, your ego may be insisting that you purchase the shiny new and more expensive car. You will then be seen as more successful and powerful with your newest acquisition or, at least, the ego tells you so. It is almost like the new car will suddenly change you for the better just because you bought it. Your older car may have operated just fine and it got you to work and to appointments without fail and it probably cost less money or may have been paid off in full. So why buy the new car? Why buy the newest, more complicated and pricey model? Why would you trade in your old reliable car, likely at a substantial cash loss, for an unknown, but expensive new one?

These are the kind of questions that a study of your ego will help you better understand. At the beginning of your ego research, you can just watch or simply become aware of its operations. Just watch when the ego pops up and starts creating grief and anxiety. Watch how active it may be day to day or hour to hour or even minute to minute depending on the circumstances. Whenever you are around people, particularly of the opposite sex, just become more aware of how often your ego influences how you talk, walk, and interact with others. Most of us are terribly concerned with always looking successful, rich, and very special. Of course, we are very special and even magnificent, but the ego seems to unbalance and focus our attention on insignificant aspects of life such as the endless quest for more useless stuff. Your essential magnificence at your core does not need the ego to function. We are so much greater than our egos. We are so much more complex and intelligent than our egos would lead us to believe. If we are unaware of the ego's actions, we will tend to fixate on such mundane matters as what kind of car to drive or what clothes to wear. After all, what does it really matter if you drive a brand new expensive car or a well maintained and reliable older vehicle?

As a Martian, I get suspicious of anyone who is displaying too many outward signs of success and wealth. Why are they working so hard to look successful? Why are they working so hard to impress everybody? I am more curious about the unpretentious person who has no need to bolster their image with depreciating assets. Have you ever heard the expression: big hat, no cattle? I am more curious with the simple, uncomplicated life that they seem to lead. Do the showy, pretentious consumers actually own outright these shiny trappings of so called success? Are they just in a lot of bad debt and simply putting on a grand show or illusion for our sake?

Issues of ego and self-esteem seem to be related in many ways and show up together in many instances. Do you judge a person by what they drive? Do you judge a person by the official schooling that they have had? Where did they grow up and what do they do for a living? All of these questions deal with such superficial aspects of the magnificent and complex person that you are interacting with. Give each person that you come into contact with the respect they deserve and watch what happens in your day. Watch your ego initially and become aware of how it operates and influences so much of your outward behavior. After this, see if you can catch and control the ego after it pops up but before it alters your actions in a negative way. You will start to feel its presence more and more as you become comfortable with just observing how it operates.

If you look at the amount of insanity currently displayed on our planet, you can be quite sure that very few people are aware of or understand the power of our egos. There is no need to fight it or even modify its actions at this point. Just watch and learn! The simple awareness of our ego's existence is a major first step in learning to work with it as opposed to trying to fight it. In my own Martian case, once I had seen the power and influence of my ego and the frequency that it appeared in my daily life, I started to respect and analyze it more closely. This moment was a major turning point for me and the light bulb in my mind glowed brightly.

I feel that this simple notice or awareness of my ego allowed me to see it not as an enemy but actually as just another complex part of my makeup that could be controlled and worked with. The more time spent watching the ego, the less it seems threatening and uncontrollable. In fact, it becomes like an old friend whose actions and responses are quite predictable. I would smile at times when my ego popped into consciousness and started his devilish routine. Sometimes, I would silently swear to myself when I noticed my ego or other peoples' egos enter into our daily interactions.

The ego is sly and clever and usually operates in the shadows below our notice. At the end of the day, do you ever find yourself wishing that you could replay and redo some of the past moments? You could replay an argument that you had with your spouse but this time the outcome would be less destructive and personal. Do you ever want to kick yourself for bad behavior, a lack of tact or anger or impatience? Generally speaking, the ego is behind all of these actions and feelings. If most or all of our suffering on this planet is related to the ego, then we must become very competent in dealing with it. We must become experts on dealing with our own egos.

At first, just watch it operate. Become aware of how it can influence your daily interactions, decisions, and even moods. As time goes by and you become less shocked by its power, small adjustments may be possible to make. Don't be too hard on yourself during this phase. Respect your body and mind enough to take the time necessary for the transition of becoming more comfortable with your own ego. The ego is not the enemy. It should be a minor part of what makes us human but, in many cases, it has become overly powerful and dominant. The ego may be used in a very minor way to help ourselves get through the day. However, I have found that basically becoming egoless is a much more productive and successful way to go thru life.

We have to learn to reign in its influence and take back control. We will become the master and the ego will become a tool to use as we see fit. I have found in my own life that the ego does much more harm than good. In fact, as mentioned earlier, I am not sure what good the ego does at all for us. The ego may help us stand out from the crowd, from being disrespected or taken advantage of, but there are better ways to get the same result. Our modern developed society has created a monster out of our egos.

People seem to be very touchy or defensive and on edge a lot of the time. Our societies have become more polarized where things are either black or white with no room to compromise or change. Does this current reality sound like the collective ego at work? As I mentioned at the start of this book, there are rarely any black or white answers or solutions when dealing with humans. In our complex human interactions, everything is a shade of grey. People are more likely to immediately argue with another rather than listen carefully and seek clarification or more details of another person's viewpoint. This type of behavior shows a lack of respect towards our fellow magnificent human beings.

I read somewhere that you have to stand up for something or you risk becoming nothing in life. You have to take a stand or have a strong opinion on many human issues. You are either with us or against us. There is no middle ground or grey area in these types of arguments. If our current society says so and so, then it must be true. My Martian feelings on these types of arguments are again a question of balance and flexibility. Your position or viewpoint should be ever changing and fluid as you gain new information. You can have a CURRENT opinion based upon your current information but that opinion will likely change as NEW information is gained. The world changes and so should your viewpoint change. We seem to take it as a personal insult or weakness if our viewpoint changes as the years go by. You will learn to pick your battles for only the most important areas of your life. These battle areas should be few and far between and carefully selected and analyzed. Most everything else is not worth arguing over even if your ego says so.

Consider a group of people at a party. One person states his opinion and position on a given topic such as politics and another person states an opposite opinion. The two people then start to escalate the energy, stress, and noise level as they each try to defend and support their views. Do you really expect to CHANGE the other person's opinion at that moment? Have you ever done so in practice? Do you know anyone who has openly changed their opinion after such a spirited discussion? Have you ever changed your own opinion either at that moment or sometime later as a result of an argument or heated conversation? Many experts suggest that we actually DEFEND our initial position more strongly even when we are presented with obvious, factual, contradictory evidence. Is this insane behaviour or what? Do you think that by arguing louder and making personal attacks on the other person will help your cause? What is being accomplished during this human to human interaction except for a lot of drama, noise, and attention for each of the participants? This is the sneaky and powerful ego at work.

Why are you fighting so hard to defend your point of view? How is it even your position to begin with? Most likely you have borrowed your present ideas from someone else and yet you feel a strong need to defend and fight for them. Your current viewpoints could have come from family, friends, or something that you read or heard recently. The current position you are arguing for was never really your position to begin with but the need to defend it is very powerful. Hopefully as you continue to learn and read new materials, your thoughts on the matter in question will evolve with the new inputs.

The main point is why are you strongly defending an idea that was not even yours to begin with and that can and hopefully will change with future information? A person could get themselves all worked up with elevated blood pressure, pulse, sweaty palms, and stress hormones flooding their bodies, all because the ego wants to aggressively fight for an opinion on a specific topic. Have you ever been involved in a multi-hour argument where no opinions change and you are physically and mentally exhausted? Nothing was accomplished except a lot of wasted energy, lots of drama and noise and a lot of wasted precious time on this planet. Do you still have the same opinion after all of those hours? Does the other person or persons still have the same position? Will you likely REPEAT this experiment tomorrow, next week, or next month? I know that I certainly did in the past.

I am still amazed at the enormous waste of energy and time trying to defend my viewpoint and convince the other person that they are wrong. This scenario of fighting for your opinion at all costs and against all common sense has become increasingly common in our developed societies. If somebody utters a negative comment about your favorite sports team, political party, or religion, then the ego battle can begin once again. Nothing is normally accomplished but lots of drama and noise. There are so many topics that are now off limits in polite everyday conversation. Why can't we just listen to another viewpoint without reacting, without ego, and without drama and noise? Just listen and let the new ideas enter your brain without fighting the process. You just might learn something new and important to your own life and for no cost at that. You will also be doing the greatest service of respecting the other human's opinion.

Our egos can get us into a lot of trouble if we remain unaware of its agenda and clever techniques to control us. Start watching for your ego to assert itself in these arguments. In fact, why ever argue again except for the most important areas of your life. Pick your battles but leave the little stuff alone. After watching the ego for a while, try to reduce its influence and power by not letting it control your emotions as much. Test yourself now and then by having a discussion and not an argument about any topic. When is it ever productive to have a full-fledged argument as opposed to a quiet exchange of differing ideas? You can certainly state your current ideas and thoughts on any given subject, but don't try to defend them so strongly. After all, do you really expect to change the other person's viewpoint at that moment? Have you ever actually succeeded at this in all of your arguments to date?

Unless the person you are talking with is basically egoless, you will likely have another argument on your hands. I have caught myself on so many occasions feeling foolish and frustrated after an intense argument. The hurt feelings and emotional pain after such an event can last a long time, even a lifetime. Next time, try having an intelligent and non-emotional discussion where you first LISTEN to the other person until they are satisfied you have done so. Allow yourself the time to listen to your fellow human sufficiently. Give yourself and him or her enough respect to slow down and just listen. Then, and only then, present your ideas without the drama/ego and try to learn something new from the exchange. Let yourself absorb the new ideas without judgment/ego. Operating with less of an ego means less talk and more listening. You have two ears to listen with and only one mouth to talk with so plan your conversations accordingly. Reign in the power and influence of your ego at these times and take back control of your mind/brain in a more relaxed and calm manner.

The ego shows up everywhere in our lives. What kind of car do you drive? What kind of house do you live in and in what kind of neighborhood? Are you wearing the latest and most expensive new fashions? How new is the car that you are driving? Is it the newest and most expensive model? Do you own the car outright or are you just making payments or have a lease arrangement? Let's look in more detail at the car you drive.

My first question as a Martian is what is the actual purpose of a vehicle? What is your car good for? If it is safe and reliable and gets you to work and back and other errands with little problem or additional expense, then it serves its purpose. Does it have to be the newest (and most expensive and probably the most complicated) for your needs? It is probably your ego that pushes you into that newer but unneeded car. It looks good and will make you appear rich and successful hopefully. But what was really wrong with your old car? It is this type of unnecessary purchasing and complicating of your life that is likely increasing your stress level and probably damaging your health (#2) and your finances/net worth or money (#3). Remember Time, Health, and Money in that order. I think the ego is the likely culprit behind these kinds of purchases, but always remember that we are complex creatures with complex behaviors. There may be other factors involved such as low self-esteem or peer pressure etc. etc. Now, of course, if the car is becoming unsafe or too expensive and unreliable to use, then look for a suitable replacement but not until those conditions are met.

There will probably become a time in your life (hopefully by implementing these money ideas) when your monthly free cash flow will be large enough to easily buy a brand new car on payments if you so please. It is usually not prudent to pay all cash for a new car because it is a depreciating asset. You can make the monthly car payments from your new and improved cash flow and achieve the same result. But first, we have to start building that pot of investments by respecting all of your financial transactions as discussed previously.

The ego wants you to try and keep up with the Jones's. The ego wants you to try and surpass the Jones's but it is not possible to do because everything keeps changing. Do you ever wonder what it would be like to have everything that you ever wanted? Think about that scenario for a long while. What would be your new purpose in life? Do you see a lot of free time and boredom perhaps? This game of life is constantly changing for better or worse. We have to take back control of the ego and think more about the reasons behind any large purchase we are contemplating in the future.

How about the house you currently live in? Back in the 1950's or so, the average square footage was around 1,000 to 1,200 and that size seemed to be just fine for young couples and even young parents. As the decades went by, the average size of our homes kept increasing at an alarming rate. The larger home naturally cost more money to buy or finance and more money to maintain and operate on a daily basis. This home probably complicated your life more with newer gadgets and features. Even your yearly property taxes will be larger because of the increased asset value.

What is pushing us to buy the much bigger house and mortgage and operating expenses? Do we really need 2,300 to 2,600 square feet of house now as opposed to the 1950's? Remember, the smaller house of the past did a fine job and served its purpose well. We have to start asking ourselves these kinds of questions. Is bigger really better in all cases? Is your financial condition going to be weakened by purchasing the larger home? Can you easily afford the increased mortgage payments and operating costs? Can you still afford them if you get sick or disabled or laid off or fired? What is happening to your stress level when you think of these possibilities? What is probably going to happen to your daily stress level after you purchase this bigger home?

Many health experts suggest that over 60% of sickness and disease are directly related to your ongoing stress levels so controlling/reducing these levels is important to your overall health and wellness. Whatever the actual percentage may be, the main point is that reducing your average daily stress level will put the odds in your favor of a good health outcome for the future. Is the purchase of the larger home worth the increase in daily stress? Will you have less time to spend with your spouse and family because of the increased financial burden? Who says that we have to own that bigger house, that newer car, or those new expensive clothes? Is it the status quo that is controlling your decisions/behaviour? How is that working out for us as a society in the developed countries? Do you think that it may be time for a change?

Start to develop the courage and pro-activity needed for a new and improved routine or paradigm of living. Take the 1st step to a new way of living on this planet. Become aware of your ego and watch it operate as you go through your day. Just watch its influence on your day to day interactions with other people or just with yourself. Watch for the drama that you create in your life. Watch for all the useless conflicts or unwinnable arguments or unlimited desire for more stuff that drives you. As hard as it is to believe, just becoming AWARE of the powerful influence that your ego has on your day to day operations will be an excellent 1st step towards eventually controlling it.

Do the Martian thing and get MAD, very mad at your current life situation or predicament. Yell and swear loudly if that works for you. It does for me. Stop the endless downward spiral by doing something different. Do not keep doing the same thing and expect different results. That process is defined as insanity. It is insane to keep doing the same things and yet expect different outcomes. It does not matter how you got to your present unhappy situation. It does not matter if your current situation is due to choices, circumstances, or just bad luck. Just get mad, get excited, get driven enough to finally take ACTION and decide at this present moment to stop the insanity.

If you are at or near the bottom of your life path, then the odds are excellent that whatever you start doing differently will pay off in spades. The odds are good that whatever you do differently will move you upwards in your life path. Same daily actions = same daily results. Different daily actions = different daily results. You will most likely have to take some kind of action or start a new habit. You will have to do something differently starting now. You can't keep doing the same things that have gotten you in trouble. Most everyone around you will likely scoff at the notion of you being able to change. But change must be possible because you are already doing it in small ways to exist in our ever changing environment. Do you have the same job as you did five years ago? Do you live at the same address or the same state as ten years ago? Do you have the same life partner, or number of dependants? Do you shop at the same stores or eat out at the same restaurants as before?

I think you get the idea. If you have ever changed jobs, houses, locations, or life partners, then you are already familiar with the ability to change. You absolutely can change and have done so already in the past. We absolutely can change, as a species, because we are doing that on most days just to cope with our changing world. I hope that you are now convinced of our inherent ability to change. However, in many instances, it seems easier to just stay the same and is probably less frightening for us.

Become an expert in something or on something and use that new skill to provide a service to others. Eventually become an expert on many different things such as nutrition, money management and investing, car maintenance, house repairs and upkeep. The list is endless and you can do it all because you have an incredible body and mind at your disposal. How exciting and how true! You are powerful and magnificent because you have the tools. There is nothing magical in this, nothing to buy, no club to join, no courses to take, but just a simple acknowledgement and simple awareness of your inherent powers to create the world that you dream of. You can do it because others have done it before you.

Are you worth the effort? Why are they so special or gifted? What do they have that is different from your equipment? Did these successful people feel that they were worth the extra effort to change their lives for the better? Are they humans with the same body and brain as you have. Probably, the only significant difference between them and you is a plan of action which creates a positive change in their world. This is very good news because you can also create a plan of action and then just do it, make the mistakes, make changes, and keep going towards your ultimate goal. Hopefully as you become aware of your ego's influence on your day to day activities, you will start to simplify your life and make a conscious effort to reduce daily complications. This simplification will allow more time or space to be created in your day and this precious extra created time is the subject of the next chapter.

TO SUM UP:

In my Martian world or way of thinking, you would:

Start to watch and become more aware of your own ego. This awareness is a good 1st step towards managing the ego as our servant and not our master.

Work towards reducing your ego and eventually becoming basically an egoless person.

We can learn to control our egos as opposed to our egos controlling us.

Watch how the ego in other humans is controlling/influencing their lives and learn from watching them.

Start paying attention to how many of your daily decisions and actions are quietly influenced by your elusive ego.

Ego reduction = stress reduction = better health and well-being.

Ego reduction = less arguing and fighting = less insane waste of your precious time on this planet.

Ego reduction in each human = less collective insanity on the planet such as world wars, global pollution, and species extinction.

Decide that you are you worth the effort to reduce and better manage your powerful and elusive ego.

CHAPTER 6: SLOW DOWN AND THINK MORE

In my Martian opinion, most people in the developed world are extremely busy, distracted, and stressed out. Trying to interact with such a human is usually a very frustrating undertaking. The status quo is continually pushing us faster and faster. If it is fast, then it must be good. If it is slower, then there must be a problem. We have 15 minute oil changes, 30 minutes or free pizzas, 5 minute speed dating and so on. Some of these things may seem an improvement but what about unnecessary mistakes with your oil change or reduced food quality with your pizza, or a bad match up with your speed date. Faster is certainly not a guarantee of better. Sure some of these things are nice but what potentially happens to quality when only speed is emphasized.

What happens to the quality of the human interaction or engagement when the time is reduced? What happens to our level of respect towards each other? What happens to our own stress levels if everything we do is rushed or glossed over? When we are rushed or pushed, then we cannot be operating at peak efficiency. Our magnificent brain/mind cannot make high quality decisions in the same way that a relaxed and properly rested brain can. Even our bodies need quality rest and nutrition to work at their best. Most things suffer when the pace is increased to a stressful level. You know when the caliber of your work suffers because you are being pushed too fast for your current skill level.

Our typical lives have become so complicated and hectic that everything seems to suffer. Our relationships tend to be shallow, short lived, and not genuine. We don't have time or take the time to develop deeper and more meaningful interactions with our fellow humans. In my Martian opinion, in our current fast paced and hectic developed world, few people care about anything or anybody except themselves. We have become incredibly apathetic towards everything outside of our little personal bubbles. Our attention spans have been reduced to mere seconds of time and the number of competing distractions has swelled in quantity. We continue to focus on our little personal worlds and perhaps immediate family members exclusively. We pay sparse attention to the other magnificent human beings that we may interact with daily. Our egos have gotten out of balance and out of control.

Remember, these other humans are also magnificent at their core just like you and I. We don't treat each other with much respect or courtesy as a general rule and the trend is getting worse in my Martian opinion. We have to start making a conscious choice to slow down and smell the roses again. Make a choice to reduce your daily complications and thereby simplify your life. We can exert control over the hectic, frantic, and desperate pace of our lives.

We have to learn to say no to certain extra and non-essential activities and obligations and instead spend more quality time developing the most important areas of our lives. Remember, time, health, and money in that order. Don't get caught wasting your precious time on this planet constantly consuming and acquiring more unneeded stuff. Stop making yourself so busy by trying to take on too much in too short a time. You ultimately control your time with your life choices. We all have the same 24 hour day and 7 day week. We just have to use our amazing human computers to better manage and control our precious time. Learn to say no to certain activities that are packing your daily schedule beyond the manageable point. Doing so will show respect for your body and brain and put the odds in your favor of a better outcome.

It seems that everyone suffers when they try to interact and engage with a hyper busy and distracted fellow human being. How much time and respect do you provide to the other people encountered in your average day? Do you slow down and engage your mail person or neighbor or bus driver or anyone who crosses your path? A simple question such as how are you doing today? Or how is your day going? This simple act shows respect, even just a little respect, towards a fellow human being who is as magnificent as you are. We all deserve this simple respect and yet I see little of it in our daily, stressed out lives currently. I make a daily conscious effort to engage all people, all races and all colors most of the time. Even Martians have a bad day every now and then.

Does this simple exercise work? What do you guess? It makes you feel good, it makes them feel good, it costs nothing to implement, and it is easy to put into practice. It is a win-win exercise to start doing now and continuing until your time on earth is over. The potential positive benefits are huge for you and the drawbacks are few if any. Are you creating friendly/helpful encounters with your fellow humans? Or are you creating a lot of potential enemies and angry fellow humans as you proceed thru your daily activities?

Studies have shown that the vast majority of us humans are not good at multi-tasking and yet we feel that we are. Most of us are not generally efficient when doing two or more things at the same time. In fact, all of those tasks will suffer in quality as we become slowly overloaded with work. Our minds/brains also suffer from too much stress and multi–tasking. We need time to identify and then analyze problems before an effective solution can be tried. When you watch TV commercials or sitcoms or even some TV movies, it is common to see highly stressed out parents trying to deal with a multitude of tasks that come at them in machine gun like fashion. Breakfast is thrown together, lunch bags are quickly packed, daily timetables are coordinated, and even the household cat or dog is taken care of all before leaving for a full day at work. When the stressed parent or parents returns after 8 hours of work and the daily commute, the same routine is repeated except with different meals this time. This tough routine is repeated at least five days a week, 50 weeks a year, and for maybe 40 years.

It is very rare to see a relaxed and slowed down family enjoying a good breakfast and conversation without the constant pressure to go faster, get more done, get more money and stuff. We are always rushing to the next great thing that should make our lives better. We often forget that we ultimately control our time and our lives. We can choose a different way, a slower more deliberate way to run our lives. We can slow down and smell the roses as they say. I even suspect that you will actually get more done at the end of the day when you slow down and think more. If you proceed at a slower and more methodical pace, you can ultimately accomplish more while seemingly doing less. Slow and steady can actually win the race because there is a lot less wasted activity and energy and a more laser-like focus on the challenge at hand.

Spending five or ten minutes to first plan out your day will pay positive dividends. When you reduce your multi-tasking and instead use a laser-like focus on individual problems as they come up, you will put the odds in your favor of having a good day. Even though you are not rushing around frantically, at the end of the day, your completed list of chores will be impressive. Slow down your pace and concentrate on the job at hand only. Focus all of your creative powers and awareness on the task at hand and nothing else until that task has been properly dealt with. You will likely come across in your daily reading, the Buddhist saying to chop wood and carry water. The simple order has far deeper meaning regarding focusing your energy, awareness, and creative powers on the job at hand only. We should do one thing well at a time and then the next thing etc. We need to slow down our lives and think more on the immediate challenge in front of us now.

In my Martian opinion, slowing down your daily pace and working more efficiently will get more done and at higher quality. The hectic, busy looking executive may seem more impressive to watch but the quiet, focused, and organized worker will likely have more accomplished at the end of the day. I remember reading about studies done with physically demanding redundant jobs. The most daily output was achieved with a lot of breaks or rests every 15 minutes or so which seemed to recharge the worker for the rest of the shift. These rested workers got more daily production than the standard shift worker who actually took fewer breaks. This idea made sense to my Martian mind because I have had similar results with my own daily output. You can accomplish more by slowing down and resting, recharging and working more efficiently. You will waste less time with unneeded activity, unfocused energy, and disorganization.

My father was a morning person and he loved getting up in the early, quiet hours before daylight to plan out his day. He worked out most of the intricate daily details so he could be as efficient as possible and get the job done. I was never a morning person and would roll out of bed, eat quickly and get to the job site. Dad and I would forever argue about the daily sequence of events. I would normally lose those arguments because he was focused, organized and aware of the best way to work the day. Dad had taken the time necessary to most effectively plan out our day. I also did not have a clue, at the time, that my elusive and unbalanced ego was creating a lot of this useless noise, drama, and conflict. Before you even begin a task, think about the problem a lot more. Don't be in a rush to just get going and do something.

What are the possible solutions and what is the simplest, most elegant one? What are the limiting factors needed to complete the job such as time, money, or expertise? The more money that is involved with a job, then the more thinking that must be done before starting. Does the work need to be done now or next week or next pay period? It is rare for me not to find a better and simpler solution when I slow down and concentrate all of my creative powers on the problem I'm facing. By slowing down and giving yourself more time and space to think and plan you will become more efficient and probably finish sooner than the old way.

Many of us just want to jump into the battle, just get at it, or just do something quickly to get the job crossed off of our daily chore list. Very often however, this initial energy spurt is just wasted and sometimes the work must be redone just to get back to the initial starting point. By giving yourself more time, you can approach any challenge in a more systematic fashion and slowly analyze what is actually causing the problem and what are the best solutions. Remember that all of this thinking, planning, and analyzing occurs in your super mind before you ever lift a tool or piece of equipment or spend any money. The pre-planning will pay huge dividends in reduced time and effort expended because you are now using your powerful creative brain more efficiently as opposed to rushing around in a panicked state just looking busy.

Slow down and de-stress your life. Slow down and simplify things. Give yourself more time and space to make better decisions. Are you worth the extra effort? Don't follow the crowd when it comes to multi-tasking and running around frantically without a plan. Slow down the pace of your life and plan and organize your efforts to get more done with much less stress to your body and mind. It can be done, others have done it with the same incredible equipment that you already have. It comes down to a simple choice to just start doing it now.

TO SUM UP:

In my Martian world or way of thinking, you would:

Start to simplify your life and daily activities by reducing the number of competing distractions.

Prioritize your day and decide what couple of things you would like to accomplish today.

Always keep in mind the three major categories of our human lives: time, health, and money in that priority.

Create more free space and free time in your daily schedule.

You can use that newly created free time to de-stress yourself and to recharge your creative computer.

Chop wood or carry water but do one thing at a time with full attention and focus on only the task at hand.

Reduce or eliminate multi-tasking because it generally does not work effectively.

CHAPTER 7: MAKE HAPPINESS AND FUN A DAILY PRIORITY

We are here for a good time but not a long time as the saying goes. That statement summarizes a possible solution to our limited time on this planet. Work towards having a good time every day. You can choose to go thru this life depressed and sad most of the time or you can choose to be happy and enthusiastic. Once again, it is up to you and apparently it is easier and much more effective being happy. It is up to you which side of your complex personality will be displayed to the world. We all have suffered and we all have past pain and regrets. Fortunately this pain and suffering is not part of a human contest to try and win. There is no 1st prize for the human who suffers the most. Your ego may try to convince you that complaining and creating a lot of noise and drama are more beneficial, but you will likely learn otherwise. Everybody hurts and everybody cries at times so you are not alone with your sadness. We all have been thru tough times, family deaths, bad childhoods, traumatic school years etc. etc. Maybe yours was worse than average or maybe it was better but it does not matter one way or the other. Let's just assume that we were all screwed up in our childhood and proceed from there. The past cannot be changed so why waste precious time thinking about it. If you decide that you are worth the effort, then there is a solution available in the present which will then likely produce a better future for you and yours.

How can it possibly help to spend your precious time in this existence depressed and feeling sorry for yourself? How much life are you willing to waste as you continually replay your past with all of its problems? Who benefits from your sadness and lack of joy? Do you get more attention or pity when you are sad and depressed? Are you able to control or manipulate others with your poor me performance? It is a miracle that you are even here with all the possible combinations of egg and sperm to choose from. Like a snowflake or a fingerprint, you are totally unique and that makes you very special. Do you agree? Is there someone out there who is a perfect duplicate of you? You are one of a kind and there will never be another one exactly like you ever. Doesn't this previous fact make you precious or magnificent? You may get little or no respect from your fellow humans, but that doesn't mean that you are not really magnificent and powerful at your core. You may feel like an insignificant cog in a huge machine, but you are really still one of a kind.

Your sadness and depression is contagious to others around you. Your happiness and enthusiasm is also contagious to those around you. Would you rather have depressed or happy people around you as you go thru your day? Your own depression and lack of zest will likely bring down the energy level of people in your vicinity. And, of course, the other way also works when you are in the company of an enthusiastic, happy and energetic human. It is easy to become caught up in the energy of such a person around you and feel more enthusiastic and happy as a result. You can become that energized person and people will respond more positively and be more helpful to you. You can shift the odds in your favor of a better interaction with fellow humans. Nothing is ever guaranteed in this life except death and taxes but you can still put the odds in your favor by choosing happiness, kindness, and respect for others.

Who benefits from your constant grumpy and bitter frame of mind? Who benefits from your constant complaining about your past, your poor childhood, bad parents, bad luck, and on and on? We all have pain, past regrets, bad decisions just like you and maybe even worse. Have you ever heard the little saying by Denis Waitley: "I had the blues because I had no shoes until I met a man on the street who had no feet"? It is all a question of perspective. Is it not? Why not go out and earn some money by providing a needed service to your neighbors, save some of that hard earned money and buy the shoes in the previous example? Be creative with your efforts and barter for the shoes or buy them at a local garage sale or buy them second hand at a goodwill type store. For just a tiny moment, think about the guy who has no feet. Suddenly your big, dramatic, and noisy problem doesn't seem all that bad after all. Most of our problems are really just a matter of perspective and how we feel about them. Just use your powerful body/brain to solve the problem and move on with no drama and no more noise about the shoes.

Speaking about buying or bartering for shoes, we can now discuss your daily happiness as it relates to that magic monthly cash flow that you can create. It probably sounds like all work and no play in regards to your initial years spent building that golden investment nest egg, but the happiness and fun will be coming soon. As your investment nest egg or portfolio increases in value, so will the free monthly dividend checks. If you continue to regularly invest your earnings as suggested earlier in the book, you will witness an almost magical mathematical process called compounding interest. You can learn much more about this amazing investment bonus in your extensive money/financial matters research.

Basically, the compounding interest or compounding growth of your portfolio will increase the total value faster than expected given enough time to do its magic. The portfolio value will start to grow in an exponential manner as opposed to a simple linear rate. The long-time investor will just notice more free monies are being created the longer that the nest egg is added to. It is like an extra bonus for investing regularly for many years. The compounding bonus starts out small in the early years but continues to grow and grow the longer that the initial investment is allowed to live so to speak. You will learn all of this and more as you become an expert with your own investment decisions. After 10 or 15 or 20 years of regular cash infusions from your work earnings, an investor could have some serious money working for him/her and generating a sizable monthly cash flow or personal pension.

The greater the percentage of your pay check that you choose to invest and of course the more money that you actually earn on a monthly or yearly basis, the larger your free monthly cash flow will become. Can you imagine an extra $1,000/month or $2,000 or $5,000 each and every month as long as you take good care of the golden goose (investment portfolio)? Can you imagine this investment program continuing for your entire working career and then being passed on to your children and grandchildren and on and on into the future? The free monthly cash flow has no limits to growth and the longer it is left to live and produce golden investment eggs, the bigger those eggs will be.

Can you imagine $10,000/month or $25,000 or more each and every month for doing nothing but staying alive and healthy so as to fully enjoy your investment windfall? Now you can guess what the 1% may be doing with their earned income or wages. Money invested on a regular basis + time = ever increasing monthly cash flow. When that monthly cash flow is large enough that you don't even need it for regular monthly living expenses, then it is time to finally start enjoying it and have some fun with your golden eggs.

If you have an extra free $500/month after all regular living expenses, then do the Martian thing and spend it all on something fun that makes you happy. It does not matter if you even waste this free money on happiness and fun because there is another $500 coming next month and next month and so on. There really is a silver lining to all of that nasty budgeting work, paying off credit card debt, becoming debt free, creating an investment portfolio and creating a free monthly cash flow, etc. etc. There will come a time when you finally get to enjoy all of your hard work and suffering from those earlier working years. You can finally be frivolous with your free monthly gifts, if you choose, and concentrate on being happy and having more fun in your later retired years. Eventually, there is a big payoff for all of your astute saving/investing over all of your earlier working years. That free money should help to put you in a positive mood more of the time which should then assist you in your future interactions with fellow human beings. A positive, enthusiastic mood is far better than any negative, angry mood.

Is there anybody or anything that benefits from your constant negative mood? Are you getting closer to the answer on this one? There must be somebody who wants this negative energy because otherwise why would you continue creating it? Think long and hard on these questions. Are you worth the effort to do so? Who benefits from your constant complaining and griping about life? What if everybody did the same constant complaining as opposed to actually doing something to rectify the problem? What kind of a world would we have then? What kind of a world do we currently have? The answer may eventually come if you do the necessary work. I hope this answer brings about a change in your old attitude and outlook on life.

Can people change? Can you change? Of course we can and we do all the time as we are forced to interact with an ever changing world. Are you exactly the same person as you were one year ago, five years ago, or ten years ago? It is really a question of effort and interest in actually changing. In my Martian opinion, it all comes down to your ego. Your ego says why should I have to change? Why can't the other person change? What's wrong with me? I must be right and the other guy must be wrong. If humans are unable to become perfect, then there must be something wrong with all of us at some point in time. So what is the big deal anyway? The answer is that you can both change if you CHOOSE to do so. That is why being egoless in this world is so helpful. Stop all the useless drama and posturing and wasting of huge amounts of energy and just let in the information, try it out, make mistakes, make changes, and move on.

Have you ever noticed how an enthusiastic person transfers energy to those people around them? The enthusiasm is a positive energy that lifts people up, gets them moving and doing things and literally brings life and energy into the situation. You can choose to bring positive or negative energy into a group or situation. The positive energy you provide can create many benefits. Some of these benefits may not be apparent initially. You are likely to help create a friendlier, more enjoyable setting and more people will tend to work with you as opposed to against you. It would be very nice to influence the number of people in your corner or on your side. It would be nice to constantly increase the number of humans willing to help and support you as you proceed through your day. You will put the odds in your favor of a better future outcome for your life. Which scenario would you prefer to help create?

Some well-read and enlightened humans say that we all eventually get what we deserve in this life. In other words, what you put out into the world tends to come right back to you. If you send out good energy, you will put the odds in your favor of receiving good energy and good results back. If you create hostility and anger from the people around you, then you will likely experience their anger and lack of help being reflected back to you. What you think about most comes about in your current reality. Your thinking creates your current life situation. What you currently think you are as a person is what you are and other people will treat you accordingly. This internal dialogue or constant thinking creates a self–fulfilling prophesy between you and the rest of the world. You think the world is bad and you constantly send out negative energy as a result and the world becomes bad for you. You think the world is generally good and you send out good energy and the world becomes good for you.

Think about it! Think about it some more. You have an unnecessary argument with a neighbor and you say things that you later regret. Likely, your ego created a lot of useless drama and noise and now you have created a person who is not on your side. This angry neighbor will now put the odds against you for a favorable future relationship. You have created an enemy so to speak and he is your neighbor. The now angry neighbor may work hard to get even with you, to restore their hurt feelings and embarrassment. His ego will not let this argument go unchallenged and he will have to get even with you somehow or sometime. Of course he/she may have a reduced ego (or be basically egoless) and the whole problem would likely just dissolve.

Otherwise your ego may have created an enemy out of your neighbour and he/she may now create a living hell for you and yours in the future to come. The once neutral neighbor can now become a bad neighbor who will make your life and living situation a constant source of tension and stress. Your neighbor's ego has been attacked and must be defended at all costs. Unless he/she happens to be an egoless type person who realizes that you may have made a mistake and it is not worth the fight with another magnificent human being. The initial argument was really not important and certainly not worth all the noise and drama and conflict that our egos love so much.

This is one way to create the self-fulfilling conditions of your existence. If your life is currently full of anger and strife and conflict and fighting, then you are likely creating some or all of it. The world is bad and is filled with bad and dangerous humans can become your experience. Just remember that you helped create this neighbor problem with your own behavior. If you send out happy, caring energy, then you will put the odds in your favor of creating happy, friendly, and supportive fellow human beings. If you send out negativity, sarcasm, and anger to other people, what do you expect in return? What kind of reception would you expect from these people? How would you react to an angry, noisy, and bitter person? How do you actually react to an uncaring, unloving, apathetic human? Do you automatically get defensive or angry? Do you try to offer help or assistance of any kind to this person? Do you even want to be around such a person? I am sure that you have found yourself in such a situation or meeting and the results are all too familiar. Can you imagine instead what it would be like to interact with a calm, caring, compassionate, and basically egoless person?

Well now, imagine reversing the roles of the uncaring, apathetic person and the neutral recipient. If you are the one who does not normally engage others in a friendly and happy manner, then how do you think you will be received? If you feel that everyone is a jerk or idiot or loser and you treat them accordingly, then what do they think of you? How are they going to treat you? If most of your day involves battling with other humans just because that is how you are, then think of the wasted energy and wasted possibilities that you are creating. When someone says that the world is bad or unsafe, think about what that person is usually sending out to the world to create their opinion. How can another person think that the world is basically good and people in general are helpful and friendly? Who is right and who is wrong? Are humans generally good or bad?

What is going on here? Which of the opposing views is more accurate? Look at some obvious facts of reality. If the world was mostly bad and people were apathetic, uncaring, and unhelpful in the past, then how could we evolve as a species and grow to such population numbers? Wouldn't we have killed each other and become extinct in the process? Experts in this field of knowledge believe that cooperation between early humans was a major factor in our future success as a species. By working together as a group as opposed to fighting and killing each other, we gained significant advantages for survival. If the world is basically bad and dangerous, then how can you explain such things as young attractive females travelling the world alone without mishap? We are talking about extensive travel by foot, bicycle, car, sail boat or any means to both developed and undeveloped countries for months or years on end? There are stories out there describing lengthy, extensive, solo trips to remote and undeveloped areas of our planet without major mishap. That reality could not exist if the world was basically dangerous and people were basically bad. With billions of humans on the planet, there are going to be some ignorant, dangerous types but the odds are apparently in your favor of encountering mostly friendly, helpful sorts and particularly in the undeveloped regions.

There are no guarantees of course, but the odds are good that a trip like that can occur without problems because most people in this world are not dangerous. This scenario is the current reality in our world in my Martian opinion. The people may be apathetic but not dangerous. The odds are good that the people you come across and interact with will not be dangerous to you. If you currently decided to do a long distance bike tour thru Iraq, Iran, and Syria, then the odds might be against you but I am not even sure of that. You would just have to do the bike tour and report back on your results. Your results would then become the current reality of a bike tour thru these countries. When you read such adventure stories, you will probably be more surprised by the many acts of kindness and hospitality that the adventurers received from total strangers. By the way, many of these strangers were dirt poor by our modern standards but still they provided assistance.

How can this hospitality be explained unless a lot of people are lying on a lot of international trips all around the world all the time? If the world is full of dangerous people, then these long distance male/ female adventurers would have been killed or molested or detained or something before finishing their travels. They should have been if you believe in the bad and dangerous worldview? No one in their right mind would even consider such a trip if it were in fact so dangerous. But the world is not because it has been done. It is amazing to read accounts of extensive hiking or biking trips in remote undeveloped areas and learn that most people are in fact helpful and friendly. I am assuming that the travel accounts are true and factual.

Most of you have experienced the death of a loved one and had regrets concerning your past behaviour towards them. You probably wished there was more kindness and respect shown to them and less useless conflict, stress, harsh words, and anger. Well, we are all slowly dying and we are all in the same boat so to speak. Being kind and courteous towards all fellow magnificent humans only makes common sense and this behavior will also benefit both the giver and receiver. It is a win-win scenario. It is easy to implement and low cost or free. The potential payoff is immense.

Let us just assume that the world is basically good and that people are mostly helpful and non- threatening. The main point that this Martian is trying to make is that you will get a much better outcome, better reality, and better life by being friendly and happy with your fellow humans. The odds will be in your favor to improve your life situation substantially. When does it ever pay to be nasty, mean, and unhelpful to your fellow magnificent human beings? Think about it. Even when you complain about bad service or products, it is more productive usually to just state your feelings without drama and personal nastiness. You can certainly be louder than normal to take advantage of the squeaky wheel process but always remember that you are interacting with a fellow magnificent human being. What you send out into the world, you will usually get back magnified. If you regularly send out negativity and conflict, then you will likely get these same things back in your daily reality. If you regularly send out enthusiasm, happiness, and respect, then you will likely get these same things back in your daily reality. Does this concept make sense to you? What you expect to happen may become a self–fulfilling reality created by your own actions and attitudes.

As a Martian, I don't think that being happy most of the time is easy. There is so much negativity and conflict bombarding each of us on a daily basis. In this crazy, insane world that we currently occupy, the challenge is huge but the effort and work must be done to change things. So go ahead and try to influence your fellow humans by your example. Being friendly pays dividends. Being nasty does not. It was work for me at first, but as the results came in and people seemed nicer, it became a habit. It is difficult to be happy in the midst of suffering and hardship but it can be done as a choice and the positive results will be obvious as time passes. If someone you meet today is sad or depressed and you engage them with a friendly comment or compliment, you will probably ease their burden and brighten their day.

What would happen if you were nasty and mean and apathetic and did not even acknowledge or engage this person? Would those actions on your part ease their burden? If it was you who was sad and depressed, who would you rather interact with? I could never understand how nasty and mean spirited humans continued to make a choice to remain so despite the common sense of an alternative personality. Happiness, kindness, and respect work on this planet while sadness, conflict, and anger do not. Starting today, make a conscious effort to incorporate daily happiness and fun into your routine and work hard towards making every day a little brighter for those around you. If you are happy, then people around you will be more likely to absorb your friendly, cooperative, and respectful energy. There is no cost involved and the potential rewards are unlimited. Time, however, is limited and ticking down, so try it today or try it now and make the choice to change for the better. You are magnificent with powerful tools at your disposal. Make the choice today to use your body and brain more effectively and start building a better life for you and your family. I hope that I was able to provide some information and guidance to make your journey upwards a little easier. You REALLY are worth the effort.

TO SUM UP:

In my Martian world or way of thinking, you would:

Make a conscious choice to be happy and stay happy regardless of everyday minor ego based conflicts.

Work on a daily basis towards being happy most of the time and having some fun.

Reduce your daily exposure to negative news on TV, newspaper, online, etc.

We all have suffered and have past pain, regrets, and conflicts, so don't become a constant complainer.

Keep your own life and its challenges in perspective to other people and places on this planet.

Eventually, you can spend that extra monthly cash on something that makes you happy and joyous for many years to come.

Start sending out more positive energy to the universe and less negative and watch what happens.

SUMMARY

In my Martian world, daily self-help reading and research will eventually reveal that the concepts of time, health, and money are in that order of priority. We all need some money to operate effectively in our developed countries. It would make sense and be ideal to get that money component taken care of as quickly as possible in your work career. We have little or no control over time but we can exert a powerful influence on our health and finances. Therefore it seems logical to work steady and hard for a five year period and concentrate on building a nest egg or personal pension which will eventually create a free monthly cash flow. Use that free monthly investment cash flow to give yourself and your family a financial cushion or buffer which should then allow for more free time and flexibility and life choices. The extra free time could then be used to think more and start simplifying your daily schedule. We can exert a powerful influence on our health via lifestyle choices, so with this financial buffer in place, we can now pay much more attention to our health and well-being.

With a more simplified lifestyle, little or no debt and good health, we can continue to think more creatively on a daily basis to fine tune our progress and start to respect our precious time on this planet. We can now use our amazing, creative computer to create a balanced approach to the significant areas of our daily lives including: spiritual, financial, educational, social, physical, nutritional, etc. Start watching your ego and its influence on your day to day activities and become AWARE of its elusive, yet powerful presence. Once you become aware of your ego and are comfortable with its existence, slowly begin the process of reducing its power and control and work towards becoming basically EGOLESS and conflict –free.

We can control our finances and we can greatly influence our health but we still have little or no control over our time in this life. You can start using your precious, limited time on this planet to slow down and THINK more, slow down and de-stress more, slow down and RESPECT your fellow human beings more. You can control the pace of your life and become either a hectic, multi-tasking, busy body full of noise, drama, and stress or a more effective, quiet, focused, and relaxed being at peace with him/her-self and respectful towards other magnificent humans and all living creatures.   Start sending out positive, enthusiastic, and helpful energy on a daily basis and watch what happens in your world.   Work towards reducing your negativity, conflict, complaining, and anger on the bad days and maybe just spend that day by yourself. Try to stay mostly HAPPY and de-stressed despite the current insane nature of our planet. Things do change and everything does change all of the time, including ourselves. The CURRENT state of our world does not have to be the FIXED or final state. We always have the power and choice to change almost anything from our individual lives, to our neighborhoods, cities, countries, continents, and entire planet. Do the Martian thing and start living each of your days as if it could be your last, stay happy and healthy as much as possible and get that golden nest egg/personal pension invested and working for you in a timely manner.

Always remember:

Fact #1:   You have an incredible self-healing body able to do physical work.

Fact #2:   You have an incredible and creative, problem-solving mind/brain for all the mental work.

Are you worth the effort to get started??

I wish you good luck and good health on your life journey.